DEEP CALLS
TO DEEP

The Bible Reading Fellowship
15 The Chambers, Vineyard
Abingdon OX14 3FE
brf.org.uk

The Bible Reading Fellowship (BRF) is a Registered Charity (233280)

ISBN 978 1 84101 731 0
First published 2015; reprinted 2016 (twice)
10 9 8 7 6 5 4 3 2
All rights reserved

Acknowledgements

A catalogue record for this book is available from the British Library

Printed and bound by CPI Group (UK) Ltd, Croydon CR0 4Y

DEEP CALLS TO DEEP

SPIRITUAL FORMATION
IN THE HARD PLACES
OF LIFE

TONY HORSFALL

Contents

Introduction

I discovered the book of Psalms in 2011.

I say 'discovered', not meaning that I was previously unaware of this much-loved Bible book, but that until then I knew only individual psalms and not the book itself. Like most people, I had my favourite psalms, which I turned to again and again. I had based retreats on Psalm 84 ('Pilgrims making progress', and led Quiet Days on Psalm 27 ('The contemplative's psalm'). I had even written a book on Psalm 23 (*Song of the Shepherd*, BRF, 2004), but I was unfamiliar with the book as a whole.

All that changed for me when, as part of the celebration of the 400th anniversary of the King James Bible, we were encouraged in church to read through the Bible in a year. As someone who handles the Bible a lot, I didn't feel I particularly needed such a challenge, but I was aware of some gaps in my Bible knowledge as well as the fact that over time I had neglected certain portions of scripture. So I decided to start my reading programme with the books I tended to overlook.

I began with Ezekiel and quickly realised why I had neglected it for so long. My mind does not grasp symbolism easily, and I find the images of wheels within wheels and flying creatures difficult to grasp. However, I dutifully finished reading the 48 (rather long) chapters and then, for light relief, turned to the book of Psalms. I decided to read backwards, starting with Psalm 150 and working my way down to Psalm 1. I would like to say there was some deeply spiritual significance in this, but there was none. It simply acquainted me with the book as a whole and gave me an appetite to know the Psalms more deeply.

This new encounter with the book of Psalms had such an impact on me that, instead of leaving them behind and moving on to other, less familiar parts of the Bible, I decided to linger there and read them again, but in the proper order. I became aware of the deep spirituality that pervades this wonderful collection of ancient prayers and hymns, and began to understand why, in some traditions, the Psalms are read repeatedly every day, often in the morning and evening. I felt I wanted to drink deeply of the life of God that is communicated to us through these inspired and beautiful words.

It seems to me that the book of Psalms, when taken as a whole, provides us with a wonderful handbook for spiritual formation. Here we see life with God as it really is. True, there is a certain distance between us and the psalms—historically, geographically, culturally and even theologically, as they reflect the old covenant between God and his people. Not everything we read sits easily with a contemporary Western mindset. They are both familiar and foreign to us, yet they continue to speak deeply to us about our relationship with God. As one Old Testament professor puts it:

As we read the Psalms, we are entering into the sanctuary, the place where God meets men and women in a special way. We will see that the conversation between God and his people is direct, intense, intimate, and above all, honest. Thus, the Psalms are a kind of literary sanctuary in the Scripture. The place where God meets his people in a special way, where his people may address him with their praise and lament.[1]

It was this intimacy with God, this raw honesty with him, that drew me to the Psalms in a fresh way. They give us words to use with God in our moments of joy and victory (praise) and in our times of despair and defeat (lament). As we read them, we can make the words our own, enter into the experience of the writer and find our own voice before God. In particular, I was drawn to the songs of lament, prayers that come from a deep place and reflect the struggle to understand what God is doing in our lives.

These 'sad songs' make up nearly a third of all the psalms and yet they are mostly neglected by the church today. Much of our spirituality is geared toward relieving our pain and finding ways to ensure happiness, success and well-being. It wants to guarantee a life of victory, of overcoming, and so its focus is always on the positive and the joy-filled. Anything that contradicts this rosy picture of cheerful certainty is ignored, denied or avoided. Those who face struggles in their walk with God are accused of unbelief or dismissed as lacking in faith or strength of character, so they often retreat into quiet isolation or drift away from a Christianity that doesn't seem to work for them. Yet struggle and challenge are necessary for authentic spiritual growth. The reality is that God sometimes does lead us down difficult paths as he seeks to draw us closer to himself and form his life within us. Far from being an invalid expression of the Christian life, suffering may well be an inescapable part of the journey of knowing God more intimately.

One of the expressions in the book of Psalms that caught my attention is the rather enigmatic phrase 'deep calls to deep' (Psalm 42:7). I am not a Hebrew scholar, and it seems that even scholars find it difficult to translate and explain the meaning of these words, but I understand them to be saying that in the deep experiences of our lives, God invites us into a deeper relationship with himself. That is why I have taken the expression as the title for this book, with the subtitle 'Spiritual formation in the hard places of life'. I believe that the book of Psalms can help us not only to make some sense of the difficult times in our lives, but also to work our way through them so that we are drawn closer to God and our faith is deepened, not weakened.

I will be looking at a selection of psalms that all use the phrase 'out of the depths' in some way. Here we can see for ourselves how God allows us to experience distress and darkness not as punishment but as transformative agents in the spiritual life. Only when we are out of our depth will we learn true dependency on God, and only when we have lost our way can we find the path that God has for us to take. As we enter into the experience of the psalmists, we shall receive valuable insights for our own journey with God.

For some readers, this material will be what they need to hear right now, and it will help them with their present distress. For others, it will enable them to process past events and come to terms with their history with God, perhaps even bringing healing and understanding. Those whose calling is to help others, either as pastoral counsellors or spiritual directors, may find insight to help them in the vital ministry of accompaniment. For all of us, I hope, it will provide wisdom that we can store away for future reference, for no one knows what the future may bring. We may be standing on firm ground today, but tomorrow may find ourselves overwhelmed by the waves and breakers.

I have asked several friends to share with you their own journey into the depths. They are all people I know well, and I have had the privilege of sharing with them and observing their lives as they have gone through the valley of deep darkness (see Psalm 23:4). Their stories are not meant to be templates for you to follow, for God deals with us as individuals and everyone's journey is unique and special. Neither are they meant to be 'happy ever after' testimonies to make you feel guilty or inadequate if your life seems not to be working out, for life is never simple or straightforward for anyone. Their intention is to give a human face to the message of this book so that we are not simply talking about theory. It is easy to sit at a desk and wax eloquent about finding God in the darkness, but much less easy to do it in daily life. These friends of mine have been there; they know what darkness is like. The stories they share are deeply moving and come to you at a price—the cost of their own suffering. Why not pray for these people as you read?

First, however, we need to do some background work in understanding the book of Psalms. This will prepare us to get the most from our study later of some individual psalms.

1
Understanding psalms

As we prepare for our study of a few chosen psalms, it will be helpful to have a basic awareness of this form of writing. This chapter is meant not as a technical introduction, but as a 'beginner's guide' so that we will be better equipped to understand the individual psalms when we come to study them.

A psalm is a poem, prayer or song that is addressed to God and expressed in the context of a faith relationship. The book of Psalms is a collection or anthology of such writings from a variety of authors and covering a long period of time, parallel to the history of Israel in the Old Testament. The book reflects the covenant relationship of ancient Israel and individual believers with their God. Psalms are also found elsewhere in the Bible, notably the song of Moses in Exodus 15:1–18, Hannah's prayer in 1 Samuel 2:1–10 and Jonah's cry to God from the belly of the great fish (Jonah 2:2–10). The majority of psalms, however, are found in the collection that we call the book of Psalms, sometimes known as the Psalter.

Psalms are, first of all, poems, presented in the distinctively Hebrew way of writing poetry. If they tell a narrative at all, it is poetic narrative in which the emphasis is not so much on the detail of the event as on its meaning and significance. Hebrew poetry makes great use of images, rhythm and sound and is designed to be read aloud. It also uses something called 'parallelism' instead of rhyme, placing two thoughts alongside each other that appear to be the same but, in fact, are slightly different. Sometimes the second line confirms the first, sometimes it expands and advances the first thought, and occasionally it contrasts and opposes it.

For instance, Psalm 2:1 begins, 'Why do the nations conspire…', and repeats the thought with '… and the people plot in vain?' The second line does not add much new information (nations = people, conspire = plot in vain), but it confirms the initial thought, expanding it just a little. The repetition gives us time to reflect on the meaning, while the balance of thought adds to the flow of the spoken word and gives it rhythm and cadence.

Psalm 103:2 begins 'Praise the Lord, my soul…', reminding us that we are called to praise God and must stir ourselves up to do so. This thought is then expanded with '… and forget not all his benefits', which gives as a reason for our praise his many benefits (blessings), and teaches us that the most likely hindrance to a life of praise is our forgetfulness and spiritual complacency.

In Psalm 1, however, the writer uses a clear contrast in verse 6 to summarise his thought. 'For the Lord watches over the way of the righteous…' is followed by a direct antithesis, '… but the way of the wicked will perish' (NRSV). Here, the righteous and the wicked are seen as opposites and the outcome of their lives as being in complete contrast.

Poetry is the language of the heart. It expresses emotion, desire, longing, passion and so on. It meets perfectly the needs of spiritual writing, allowing deep feelings to be expressed through metaphor and word pictures, but lacks the clarity and sharpness of a legal document. It is important to remember this when we are reading psalms: we are reading poetry, not doctrine. Psalms are best suited to reflection and meditation, thinking deeply about issues and coming back to the same text again and again. Their poetic shape helps us to express our own emotion and unlock our hearts in the presence of God.[2]

Secondly, psalms are prayers, expressing a heartfelt relationship with God. Here we listen to grateful responses to the goodness of God, as well as anxious pleas and urgent cries for help. What strikes us immediately is that they are directed towards God and they are spoken with honesty and candour. They offer to God sincere thankfulness and express genuine trust and confidence, but are also a vehicle for question, complaint and even grievance. This can be disturbing to our Christian (and Western) view of prayer, as we tend to value respect, dignity and a careful choice of words when addressing the Almighty. Such 'niceness' and 'appropriateness' is often disturbingly lacking in the Psalms.

The fact that the psalmists were not weighed down by a need for politeness is due largely to the fact that they were praying out of a secure relationship with God, based upon his covenant with Israel. They therefore felt free to be open and honest with God. Indeed, any real relationship requires such direct communication, rather than either passive resignation or active rebellion. As David Cohen writes:

This articulation of distress through psalms needs to be viewed in the broader context of covenant. Because the people of Israel were God's covenant people they had permission, as individuals and as a community, to pray to God about their distress. Praying about distress was viewed as an appropriate and normal activity within the context of the divine–human relationship.[3]

Perhaps one of the lessons we can take from reading the psalms is that we can dare to be real before God and have no need to hide behind a spiritual façade built upon good manners. Intimacy and honesty belong together.

Psalms are also songs, and this reminds us of their use in worship. Clearly, some were intended for a private setting and individual use, but many were written to be performed in a congregational context. They give instructions for singers and musicians, including the titles of tunes to be used, and the presence of an orchestra is indicated: strings, percussion and wind instruments are all mentioned. Psalms 42 and 43 are linked together by a chorus or refrain (42:5, 11; 43:5), which gives it the feel of a song, and we can easily imagine Psalm 136 (with its repeated refrain of 'His love endures for ever') being sung responsively by a congregation on a great occasion of national rejoicing.

More than 70 psalms are attributed to David, 'Israel's singer of songs' (2 Samuel 23:1, NIV 1984). His musicianship was well known, and many of the songs of Israel originate with him. His great desire was that the temple would be a place of celebration and musical excellence, and to this end he made elaborate preparations for a tradition of worship to be established (see 1 Chronicles 15:16, 19–24; 16:7; 25:1–7). The annual festivals of Israel, the appointment of kings, sabbath days and covenant renewal times may have been the settings for much of this worship, as well as the daily temple ritual. After the return from exile, leaders such as Ezra and Nehemiah were quick to restore the pattern of worship established by David to the newly returned nation (Ezra 3:10; Nehemiah 12:45–46), and may even have added to the repertoire.

Much contemporary worship is expressed almost exclusively through the medium of praise, with loud music accompanying the enthusiastic singing of joyful anthems and rousing choruses that express victory and the promise of overcoming. There is an important place for this style of worship, of course, for God inhabits the praises of his people (see Psalm 22:3, KJV). Indeed, the book of Psalms is often rightly given as the basis for such uninhibited expression and bold assurance, with its constant exhortation, 'Let everything that has breath praise the Lord' (Psalm 150:6). At the same time, we must ask if there is also a place today for the songs of lament contained in this wonderful book. How are we to help those people to worship whose lives are racked with pain and whose hearts are broken through suffering? Is there a voice for them? Are there also times when, as a community of God's people, we want to express before God our sorrow and anguish over the suffering of the world? Perhaps this is where a careful use of the psalms of lament can help us to broaden the appeal of our worship.

Traditionally, Old Testament scholars were concerned to identify the historical context in which individual psalms were written, and, while this context can be ascertained reasonably accurately for some of David's psalms, with most others it cannot be done. Indeed, many of the psalms seem to be deliberately vague and non-specific, as if to make their application easier to circumstances in the future.

Scholarly attention has also turned to identifying the type or genre of the different psalms, and classifying them according to their characteristics into various groupings. There is by no means any agreement about what exactly these types are, nor any consensus on how to classify each individual psalm. Some psalms are easy to place, others less so; some psalms have several potential identities, and there is no definitive list. While it is helpful to group some particular psalms by genre, we must remember that they were not written according to a predetermined classification: any such identification has been placed upon them by scholars, in an attempt to make sense of them.

I will give here my own understanding of the seven most commonly suggested classifications, seeking to make them as accessible as possible for non-technical readers. A fuller breakdown can be found at the back of this book ('Classification of various psalms') and more detailed descriptions are given in the books cited in the Bibliography.

Most scholars are agreed upon two main psalm types: praise and lament. *Praise psalms* take the form of hymns, easily recognised by their exuberant praise of God. Some of them are declarative, celebrating his mighty acts, while others are descriptive of God, focusing on the attributes revealed by his acts. Often there is a call to enthusiastic worship, and reasons for praise are given. God is joyfully celebrated as creator and redeemer. It is easy to see how these psalms would have been used in temple worship and on formal occasions.

In contrast to these joyful expressions of praise are the *psalms of lament*, songs that come from the depths of the experience of an individual or the nation. They are heartfelt cries for help, addressed to a God who seems sometimes to be either absent or uncaring. They arise from situations of sickness and distress, persecution and false accusation, even sin and failure, and contain strong expressions of complaint towards God and hostility towards the 'enemy', whoever that may be. In most cases, by the end of such psalms, the difficulties have been resolved, at least in part, and the psalms tend to finish with expressions of faith and confidence in God. We can imagine them being used at times of national crisis, on the Day of Atonement or during times of individual need.

Between these two extreme expressions of faith, we have *psalms of thanksgiving*, the response of a grateful person whose cry of lament has been heard. These psalms look similar to the hymns of praise, except that there is usually a restatement of the lament that has been resolved. Again, they can be both personal and national in character. Closely connected to the psalms of thanksgiving are the *psalms of trust and confidence*, where the writer expresses belief in the power and goodness of God, despite the presence of threat. This belief may be expressed before, during or after a crisis. When we put these groupings together, we can see that they reflect the kind of 'upward' movement that often takes place in the spiritual life: from lament, through petition and trust, to thanksgiving for deliverance, and then to hymns of praise in which God is extolled as his people's ever-present saviour and deliverer.

Some other psalms are *psalms of remembrance*, looking back at the history of Israel and drawing lessons from God's dealings with his people. They often refer to the exodus as a formative and foundational event in Israel's salvation history, and to the establishment of the Davidic covenant as the basis for their continuing hope in God. A few psalms are classified as *wisdom psalms*, reminding Israel of the way God wants them to live their lives and of the contrast between the righteous and the wicked. Some have a strong focus on the Torah, the law of God being the basis of all true wisdom.

A good many psalms are described as *kingship* or *royal psalms*, and, for some scholars, they represent the main theme of the entire book. Often, their focus is on the human king of Israel—either David or his descendants. They recognise that the king rules on behalf of God and, therefore, prayer is made for him. In other kingship psalms, however, the attention is on God as king, and here we see a messianic element (and a prophetic link to Christ). The purpose of these psalms is to take the reader's attention away from human kingship, with its failure and weakness, turning it towards the one true ruler who never fails and is always good and just.

How did the psalms come to be written? Well, some were the product of individual spirituality and later found their way into more general use. Others were written by professional temple musicians for specific occasions in the worship life of Israel. Eventually they were brought together into the collection of psalms that we have today, and how that happened will be the subject of the next chapter. Each psalm can be read as an individual piece of literature, but it also has its place within the Psalter; and, just as each individual psalm has a message, so too does the book as a whole.

2

Understanding the book of Psalms

When most of us read the book of Psalms, we focus on individual psalms, some of which we know very well because they are easy to read and understand, some of which are much less familiar because they are harder to grasp and sometimes express sentiments that make us uncomfortable (such as 'break the teeth in their mouths, O God', Psalm 58:6). Some psalms are at home in a contemporary worship setting and are used often, while others seem to have no place at all and are neglected. Consequently we have a good knowledge of a few psalms but only a minimal grasp of the book as a whole.

What is more, there are 150 psalms, some of which are quite long, and this makes for a sizeable book which is a challenge to a reader's attention span and memory. Many psalms sound much the same, being quite repetitive, with little distinction between them. Furthermore, there appears to be no way of grasping a coherent theme in the book. There is no narrative binding the psalms together, no chronological order to follow, and no specified grouping to give them shape or form. If the book of Psalms can rightly be called the hymn book of the temple, it is like no other hymn book we know. Apart from the numbering, it follows no pattern or order that is easily discerned, no system or plan. The arrangement seems haphazard and shapeless. True, the psalms are divided into five books (1—41; 42—72; 73—89; 90—106; 107—190) but, at first sight, this grouping too seems random and without any obvious motive. It may be an attempt to parallel the five books of the Pentateuch (Genesis to Deuteronomy), but how it does so is unclear.

Recent scholarship on the Psalms has concentrated on trying to understand how the individual psalms came to be brought together, and on seeking to discover whether there is, in fact, an overall plan or purpose behind the apparently haphazard arrangement. Both approaches can help our understanding of individual psalms as well as enriching our appreciation of the message of the book as a whole.

Many people assume that all the psalms were written by David, and, of course, 73 of them are attributed directly to him, sometimes with a superscription giving a specific setting from his life story. Other authors are also mentioned, though—Moses, Solomon, Jeduthun, Heman, Asaph and the son of Korah—so David is clearly not the sole writer. Some psalms are not attributed to any author: they could have been written by anyone and are known as 'orphan psalms'. There is also a wide historical background to the psalms, some coming apparently from the time of the exodus (Psalm 90), and others from the exile in Babylon (Psalm 137). Clearly no one person could have been responsible for the whole book. How, then, did they come to be brought together?

It seems likely that Books 1 and 2 come from the time of David, the period when the monarchy came into being, and reflect his own devotional life and the making of God's covenant with him. They also reflect his interest in providing a tradition of worship in Israel, and his concern for the temple that Solomon, his son, would later build. The connection with him is suggested by the ending of Book 2: 'This concludes the prayers of David son of Jesse' (72:20). Either David himself or an unknown editor, then, was responsible for this first compilation.

Books 3—5 were added at a much later date, probably during or after the exile, by an unknown editor or editorial team. C. Hassell Bullock suggests that the first stage of this process brought Books 1—3 together and that they reflect the hopes and fears of Israel in the period leading up to the fall of Jerusalem in 586BC.[4] During the exile and the period of the return from Babylon, further collection and editing took place, leading to the addition of Books 4 and 5: thus, 'with the stroke of a genius, the Psalter receives its final shape'.[5] The identity of this 'genius' remains unclear but, in my own mind, Ezra, the priest and teacher of the law of Moses—a man devoted to the study of the law and expert in all things concerning the commands and decrees of God—must be a prime candidate (Ezra 7:1–11). His overriding concern was for the rebuilding of the temple and the reintroduction of its worship in line with the guidelines given by David, and he would certainly have had an interest in restoring the psalms to public life, as well as the ability to put this restoration into practice (Nehemiah 11:22–23; 12:8–9, 24, 43, 45).

If this gives us an idea of how the psalter came into being, what can we learn about its purpose? If, as seems likely, its final shaping took place in the post-exilic period, the book is likely to reflect the concerns of Israel at that time. We can identify three major issues that the book of Psalms may well have been designed to answer.

First, the big-picture view of the Psalms suggests a movement from lament through to praise, not just in individual psalms but in the book as a whole. Put very simply, and in general terms, the songs of lament are in the earlier part of the book, while the songs of praise occur more often towards the end. Indeed, the book ends with a great crescendo of praise, in the 'Hallelujah Psalms' (146—150). Thus, as we read consecutively through the Psalms, we are taken on a journey from darkness into light, a journey that reflects a timeless movement in the spiritual life, and a message that would have given hope to those in exile or newly returned.

James Mays comments:

As you survey the arrangement of the book, a major shift is discernible as one moves from beginning to end. In its first section the book majors in prayers in individual and corporate voice. But with the Psalms numbered in the nineties a shift to hymns, the genre of praise, occurs... The entire anthology was given the name Tehillim, *an abstract plural that means Praise. By its movement, conclusion and title the book in its shape defines all its contents, the prayers and instruction, as the praise of the Lord... The making of the Psalter turns out to have been a project to put praise on the scriptural agenda.*[6]

Another theme begins to emerge as we survey the whole landscape of the Psalter. The book appears to be designed to answer the two central questions that had arisen to disturb the faith of the godly in Israel: first, why do the unrighteous seem to prosper and the righteous suffer, and second, how can Israel be defeated, given God has chosen Jerusalem and made a covenant with David? These two questions emerge from the challenge to Israel's basic theological understanding that was caused by its experience as a nation, and they account for much of the pain and anguish expressed in the songs of lament. In the process of lament, the people of Israel are called to rethink some of their cherished assumptions and to review their relationship with their God.

The structure of the book deliberately places Psalm 1, with its conviction that the righteous will flourish while the wicked will perish, at the head of the collection. Then, equally deliberately, comes Psalm 2, with its declaration of the rule of God over the nations and his choice and appointment of his king in Zion. These fundamentals are, of course, true, but they are apparently contradicted by Israel's circumstances and distorted by too simplistic an understanding of what they mean. As we read through the book, we encounter individuals wrestling with this seeming inconsistency and finding their own way through the darkness. Likewise, the nation as a whole had to wrestle with its theology until a deeper understanding emerged. This is why the Psalms continue to be so spiritually formative—and the lament psalms, in particular, so helpful—because we also wrestle with questions of faith. They provide us with a map and some travellers' tales for our own journey of understanding.

A third insight to emerge as we consider the whole book is that the theme of kingship seems to be a thread running throughout, especially the notion that God is king. Perhaps, in the face of the loss of their country, the destruction of their capital city and its temple, and the overthrow of the monarchy, Israel may have been concentrating too much on a human Davidic king when their hope should have been in Yahweh, the divine king. The kingship psalms are scattered throughout the book, and, while they are in no way critical of the Davidic monarchy, there is an increasing emphasis towards the end of Book 4 and especially in Book 5 on the rule of God and the expectation of the coming Messiah. It is as if Israel is being told, in the light of the demise of the

Davidic monarchy, 'Focus your attention on God, the Sovereign Lord, not on any earthly ruler.' The time of exile and absence from the land is meant to be a period of spiritual refinement and purification, a time to strip away false allegiances and unhelpful attachments. Again, if we have ears to hear, the Psalms will speak to us in our own struggles about where our allegiance lies, who is in control of our lives and whether or not we truly believe that God is sovereign.

'What lessons would the consecutive reader learn from the Psalter?' asks Geoffrey Grogan in his commentary. 'Certainly the importance of God's rule,' he continues, 'but also that he does not always explain his ways, so that the reader must learn to trust and hope in him as well as to obey him.'[7] When we wrench individual psalms out of their wider context, we are in danger of missing some of their meaning and losing some of their impact. By looking at the bigger picture painted for us by the book of Psalms, however, we will be in a better position to understand and learn from the particular psalms that feature in this study.

3

In the dark valley

We have seen that one category of psalm is the lament, an honest and open cry to God for help in the midst of distress, and that a third of all the psalms can be classified as lament. We have seen also that the book of Psalms as a whole can be said to reflect the journey from lament through to praise, a journey that reflects a movement that takes place in the spiritual life as we encounter pain and suffering in our own lives. It is during these periods of darkness and turmoil that God is at work in us, and, in the setting of our deep distress, invites us into a deeper experience of himself. If we choose to respond to this invitation, we discover that suffering can have a transformative effect upon us, changing us within and making us deeper people. Slowly, we ourselves can move from lament to praise.

In the psalms of lament, we discover a voice for our own faith struggles and begin to find hope in the midst of our despair. David Cohen writes:

Perhaps it is these psalms which resonate most deeply with our humanity. They voice a sense of brokenness and vulnerability, common in human experience, as they complain to, and protest before, God… Lament psalms are one resource which offers a pathway towards this healthy engagement with distress.[8]

It is for this reason that we will be looking at a few carefully chosen psalms of lament: we need to be able to make this 'healthy engagement' for ourselves if we are to make progress during periods of darkness in life, without stumbling.

Anyone who has a keen interest in spiritual formation will be aware of the 'life–death–resurrection' pattern that seems to be at the heart of all spiritual growth. It can be compared to going down into a dark valley, pausing, and then coming up again on the other side, transformed. Perhaps David had this in mind as he reflected on his own experiences in Psalm 23:4, a verse that can be translated as 'Even though I walk through the valley of the shadow of death, I will fear no evil, for you are with me.' Here we see the four main elements that interact in the drama of lament: the person of faith, the reality of darkness in their experience, the awareness of danger and opposition, and the protective presence of the good shepherd, leading them through the valley to the other side.

The 'life–death–resurrection' progression is seen supremely in the life of Jesus. Philippians 2:6–11 paints an amazing word-picture of his descent into the dark valley and his triumphant ascent on the other side to his place of exaltation. His 'life' is in heaven, where he shares equality with God. This is his starting point, his normal mode of existence. Then the journey downwards begins, through the process of emptying himself (letting go of his position and status, taking the form of a servant, and becoming human in the incarnation) and humbling himself (becoming obedient and willing to die, even in shameful crucifixion), until he is in the place of 'death'. There he waits until 'resurrection' happens and he is brought back to life, then exalted back to God's right hand, victorious and triumphant as the ascended Lord who has accomplished the Father's will.

The movement of 'life–death–resurrection' that we see in

Jesus provides a template for understanding so much of what happens in the life of the believer who wants to grow in grace. Christ's experience is the model for our own journey, and he spoke of it to his disciples in John 12:24: 'I tell you the truth, unless a kernel of wheat falls to the ground and dies, it remains only a single seed. But if it dies, it produces many seeds.' Here, the worlds of nature and of farming teach us the same principle. A grain of wheat can hold on to its 'life' but it will remain alone and produce nothing. If it falls into the place of darkness within the earth, it will 'die', but, as it does so, a 'resurrection' will take place and the life within the seed will be released, leading to fruitfulness and a multiplication of many more seeds.

This same 'life–death–resurrection' principle is operative in the psalms of lament. One Old Testament scholar who has drawn attention to it is Walter Brueggemann. His approach to the study of the psalms reflects a more pastoral purpose than others, and his focus is on the spiritual dynamic that the psalms reveal, rather than on their classification. He suggests two decisive movements in the life of faith that are seen in the psalms. One is from a settled position or orientation into a time of chaos and disorientation. The other is from the context of disorientation into a new orientation. These two movements correspond to the 'life–death' and 'death– resurrection' pattern in the life of Christ. Brueggemann concludes that 'the shape and dynamic of the Psalms can most usefully be understood according to the theological framework of crucifixion and resurrection' and he says that 'the voice of lamentation in the book of Psalms is indeed the voice of the Crucified One'.[9]

Brueggemann's scheme therefore identifies psalms that reflect these movements in the life of faith and the seasons of life they represent: seasons of well-being when everything is smooth and we can see that God is in control (orientation); seasons of hurt, alienation, suffering and death when we feel anger and resentment towards God, expressed in the cry of lament (disorientation); and seasons of surprise when joy breaks through the despair, and light replaces the darkness (reorientation). This movement between the seasons is transformational, though never easy and always involving pain and surprise. Brueggemann concludes that 'the life of faith expressed in the Psalms is focused on two decisive moves of faith that are always underway, by which we are regularly surprised and which we regularly resist'.[10]

Psalms of orientation express a stable situation in which God is experienced as good, reliable and trustworthy. Life as seen here is not troubled or threatened but is well ordered, as God intended it to be under his sovereign control. Creation reflects the greatness and glory of its creator, who is kind and generous to all. The world is safe, predictable and certain, and the life of faith is lived under the blessing of God. The feeling is that 'the boundary lines have fallen for me in pleasant places' (Psalm 16:6) and there is much for which to thank God. God's law is seen as the foundation of this stability. The righteous prosper and the wicked are punished, so a life lived according to the wisdom of God will be a life that prospers. If we fall ill, there is healing; if we are poor, God provides for us; when we are in trouble, he delivers us; if we have enemies, we will overcome them. Prayer is a joyous song of thanksgiving.

Psalms that reflect this orientation (as suggested by Walter Brueggemann) are 1, 8, 14, 15, 19, 24, 33, 37, 104, 112, 131, 133 and 145.

Psalms of disorientation reflect the dawning realisation

(which comes to us either slowly or abruptly) that life is not always either safe or good. A dismantling of the secure, known world takes place in the light of the grim realities of life, which is both frightening and disturbing. We enter a period of chaos; we go down to the depths; we are in the place of death. Sometimes God is silent and inactive and seems far away, even though we have done nothing wrong. Our prayers go unanswered and there is no healing. God's people are defeated, while the wicked seem to prosper and triumph. Questions arise (Why? How long? When?), anger is expressed, blame is apportioned and guilt is felt. Darkness engulfs us and hope is lost. Prayer becomes a lament, an anguished cry from the heart.

Psalms that reflect disorientation (as suggested by Brueggemann) are: 13, 32, 35, 49, 50, 51, 73, 74, 79, 81, 86, 88, 90, 109, 130, 137 and 143.

Psalms of new orientation reflect a dramatic change in perspective. Even in the psalms of disorientation, we usually catch a glimmer of light breaking through. When it seems that all hope is lost, we are surprised by the touch of God, lifting us out of the 'pit' and planting our feet on firm ground again. This movement is entirely one of grace, for it cannot be predicted or manipulated. It is always inexplicable and unexpected and can only be attributed to the intervention and timing of God. It does not involve a return to the old, stable situation that existed before the crisis, for, as Brueggemann points out, there is no going back. Rather, what emerges is a new relationship with God—deeper, richer and fuller than before. This newness is expressed by a new song of praise, thanksgiving and testimony, a song sung with greater depth and more humility than previously. Confidence in God has returned, and prayer becomes praise again.

Psalms that reflect reorientation (as suggested by Brueggemann) are: 23, 27, 29, 30, 34, 40, 47, 65, 66, 92, 93, 96, 97, 98, 99, 100, 103, 113, 114, 117, 124, 135, 138, 146, 147, 148, 149 and 150.

Of course, life is never as tidy as any theory would suggest, and the movements that Brueggemann describes are not always clear-cut or sharply defined, as he himself recognises. Yet, the flow of life is never static and over the course of a lifetime we will move into and out of orientation several times. It is helpful to have a model to work with, to help us understand something of what God may be doing, and where we may be on our journey.

The shape of this book will now follow the pattern of orientation–disorientation–new orientation. We will begin by looking at Psalm 145, which describes the settled situation of orientation, when all is well with the world and everything as it should be. We will then look at four psalms that describe different types of disorientation and take us to different depths of darkness. Psalm 130 brings before us the reality of failure and our need for forgiveness. Psalms 42 and 43 belong together as one composite song, and help us explore the darkness that is depression, arising from the grief of disappointment and loss. In Psalm 69 we go deeper still, encountering the pain of unjust suffering and being helped to face up to the anger we feel but often do not express. Psalm 88 takes us to the deepest and darkest place of all, where the writer feels abandoned by God. Finally we will explore Psalm 30, a prayer written from the perspective of reorientation, of one who has come through the valley and has emerged on the other side. Lessons have been learned, grace has been received and transformation has happened.

These particular psalms have been chosen because they

help us to get a good feel for the journey through the valley. I could have chosen many other psalms to reflect the journey of transformation, and life offers many more expressions of disorientation than the ones covered here. However, the ones chosen for attention should be relevant and sufficient to mark out a path for us—a way through the woods, so to speak, for our onward journey with God.

4

Psalm 145:
An alphabet of praise

Our journey through selected psalms begins with Psalm
145, a song of praise reflecting a period of stability, certainty
and blessing, which characterises the phase we have called
'orientation'. It describes what we might call the 'normal'
experience of God's people when they live under his bountiful
care and protection and life is good and as it should be. It is
important that we have a clear grasp of what is normative,
for this gives us a starting point, a base line to work from and
come back to, and an anchor for our souls when times are
tough. And this is the norm, that God's people are blessed by
him in order that they may be a blessing to others (Genesis
12:2–3; Psalm 67:1–7).

Psalm 145 is ascribed to David, and it may well have been
written by him or by another person in the tradition of psalm
writing that he began. There is no story line to this song, no
historical references by which we can identify the author.
It is an acrostic, a carefully crafted poem in which each line
begins with a different letter of the Hebrew alphabet, in
chronological order. Its purpose seems to be to give us an
A–Z of who God is and what he is like, and to describe life
in covenant relationship with him. It may well have been
written with a catechetical purpose in mind, as it makes an
ideal primer for anyone wanting to get to know God better.

Opening praise of God the King (vv. 1–3)

I will exalt you, my God the King;
I will praise your name for ever and ever.
Every day I will praise you,
and extol your name for ever and ever.
Great is the Lord and most worthy of praise;
his greatness no one can fathom.

We have seen already that, in the book of Psalms, praise is the basic ingredient in the worship of God, and here we are reminded that the disciplined declaration of God's greatness is fundamental to the life of faith. Praise always comes first. The writer speaks out of a deep personal relationship with God ('my God the King') to exalt him, delighting in his name or character. This he is determined to do on a daily basis and throughout his life ('for ever and ever'). God is great and therefore deserves to be greatly praised—that is, with enthusiasm and zeal, never half-heartedly or unfeelingly.

So it is that God's people can be expected to adopt praise as a way of life, and for most of the time they have good reason to do so; it is no hardship. At the same time, we must beware of reducing God to the level of our human under-standing, for 'his greatness no one can fathom' (v. 3). This thought provides us with an important insight, for the confu-sion we sometimes experience in following God stems partly from the fact that we cannot always understand what he is doing. We would like to reduce him to the safe confines of our formulas and creeds, but often he will not fit in the boxes we have mentally constructed for him. Authentic praise will therefore seek to acknowledge that God is not only great, but greater than all our ideas of him.

God the great Creator (vv. 4–7)

One generation will commend your works to another;
they will tell of your mighty acts.
They will speak of the glorious splendour of your majesty,
and I will meditate on your wonderful works.
They will tell of the power of your awesome works,
and I will proclaim your great deeds.
They will celebrate your abundant goodness
and joyfully sing of your righteousness.

The individual singer of the opening verses is now placed within the context of community praise and, indeed, inter-generational praise, for celebration of God's greatness is to be an ongoing feature of the life of God's people. The discipline of praise, and the reasons for doing it, are passed from one generation to another. Although the term 'Creator' is not specifically used of God in these verses, they seem to refer to his creative activity in the world (notice especially the expression 'all he has made' in verse 9). The focus is on his wonderful works, his great deeds and his mighty acts, not simply in a historical sense (what he did then) but with an awareness of his ongoing involvement in the life of his people (what he is doing now). Thus they can speak, tell, commend, proclaim, sing and celebrate his character and his achievements together.

This buoyant confidence in God is a feature of life when we are in the orientation phase. There are times when it is easy to see what God is doing in the world, and we have personal testimony to give of his activity in our lives and his inter-vention on our behalf. God's people can be expected therefore to revel in his greatness, delight in his creation and experience his power. We live in a God-filled world and, if we have eyes to see, we can recognise his handiwork all around us.

God the gracious Lord (vv. 8–9)

The Lord is gracious and compassionate,
slow to anger and rich in love.
The Lord is good to all;
he has compassion on all he has made.

In many ways, this is the heart of the psalm, for here we have Israel's basic understanding of God, given to Moses during the exodus and in response to his prayer, 'Now show me your glory' (Exodus 33:18). God came down in the cloud, passed in front of Moses and proclaimed his name—which means that he revealed his character and nature, for his glory is in who he is, not simply in what he does. These words from the psalm are not the full version of what was said to Moses (see Exodus 34:6–7); they are a summary and a central theological assertion of what God is really like, which the faithful held on to. The same or similar words are often used in the Psalms (see 86:15; 103:8; 111:4; 112:4) and occur elsewhere at key moments in Israel's history (Numbers 14:18; Nehemiah 9:17; Joel 2:13; Jonah 4:2).

These verses describe six major characteristics of God, each of which inspires both confidence and trust for those who believe in him. He is gracious, merciful, patient, loving, good and compassionate. In particular, these qualities describe the way he relates to human beings. They are relational qualities rather than abstract notions or philosophical concepts. He is a God who loves us and can be relied upon to deal kindly with us. While this knowledge is a strong reassurance to us, it also creates expectations in us about how he will treat us. It is when these expectations are broken that we find ourselves disoriented and bewildered.

God the glorious King (vv. 10–13a)

All you have made will praise you, O Lord;
your saints will extol you.
They will tell of the glory of your kingdom
and speak of your might,
so that all men may know of your mighty acts
and the glorious splendour of your kingdom.
Your kingdom is an everlasting kingdom,
and your dominion endures through all generations.

Once again, we see that praise is central to the life of faith, and here the basis for such thanksgiving is in the benevolent rule of God. Kingship is a major theme of the Psalms, and, as we have seen, the editor's purpose in bringing the collection together may well have been to remind Israel that it was God who reigned as their king, not some fallible earthly ruler, even one who was descended from David. In these verses, the focus is on the kingdom of God, its glory and power (v. 11), the associated splendour (v. 12) and its permanence in contrast to the transience of earthly dominions. Such a kingdom is to be celebrated and made known (v. 11), and such a king is to be worshipped and adored, especially given his character as described in verses 8–9. His rule is to be welcomed and his reign acknowledged.

This belief in the sovereignty of God provides much comfort and assurance to God's people. The world is not out of control or at the mercy of malevolent forces, but, rather, is subjected to the rule of God. He may have enemies but they are not his equals and they will be overcome. Creation may show the effects of the fall in its wildness and destructiveness, but he remains Lord over all. No matter what is happening around us, we can be confident and need not be afraid, for, in the repeated chorus of Psalm 46, 'The Lord Almighty is with us; the God of Jacob is our fortress' (vv. 7, 11). Thus, God's people can expect to see his rule demonstrated in their earthly lives and to know his power at work on their behalf. This is how things should be, with God in control and his people unafraid.

God the generous provider (vv. 13b–16)

The Lord is faithful to all his promises
and loving toward all he has made.
The Lord upholds all those who fall
and lifts up all who are bowed down.
The eyes of all look to you,
and you give them their food at the proper time.
You open your hand
and satisfy the desires of every living thing.

The faithfulness of God was implicit in the description in verses 8–9 but it is highlighted here as it provides yet another basis for the confidence of God's people. God's covenant love is expressed in faithfulness, and his faithfulness is shown in the fact that he keeps his promises and upholds his people (v. 13). While human beings are weak and prone to fall, God remains constant in his love for them and compassionate in his response to their need. Time and again he comes to their aid (v. 14), doing for them what they cannot do for themselves. What is more, in his faithfulness he provides for them materially, giving them their food and meeting their deepest needs. This open-hearted God is also open-handed in his generosity and practical support of his children. Although the term 'Father' is not used of God in this psalm, he certainly acts with fatherly care.

This means that God's people can live securely and at peace because their lives are being watched over by a generous provider. It is normal for them to live in dependence upon God and to see him meet their every need. If they fall, he will lift them up; when they are in want, he will supply their need. He will be true to his word and fulfil his promises, and his love will never fail. Life with God implies his favour and blessing, and we can say, 'The Lord is my shepherd, I lack nothing' (Psalm 23:1).

God the guardian-protector (vv. 17–20)

The Lord is righteous in all his ways
and loving toward all he has made.
The Lord is near to all who call on him,
to all who call on him in truth.
He fulfils the desires of those who fear him;
he hears their cry and saves them.
The Lord watches over all who love him;
but all the wicked he will destroy.

The justice of God is another aspect of his character that gives confidence to his people. Because he is both righteous and loving, they can safely commit their way to him and know that he will act justly (v. 17). Firstly, he is near to them—not distant and aloof, detached or indifferent, but close in the sense of being fully aware and understanding of their needs (v. 18). Secondly, he listens to their cries for help and answers their prayers, being aware of their longings and always ready to come to their aid (v. 19). Thirdly, he watches over them, attentive to their circumstances, protective in his loving concern. Thus his people can live securely. God loves them, and they love him in return.

Not only this, but he also ensures that there is justice in the world. While the righteous will be blessed, the wicked (those who reject God and his law, live self-centredly and hurt others) will be judged accordingly. A moral universe demands accountability and, without such ultimate justice, evil would triumph. The righteous know that God will act to uphold his law. The God who revealed himself to Moses is not only loving, but also just (Exodus 34:6–8). He will punish those who do wrong.

This sense of living in a well-ordered universe, where the righteous prosper and the wicked are punished, was fundamental to Israel's understanding of God. It is expressed in much of the Wisdom literature, as well as many of the psalms—in particular, Psalm 1, which sets the tone for the whole book: 'For the Lord watches over the way of the righteous, but the way of the wicked leads to destruction' (1:6). Such a belief helps us to make sense of things and to believe in the validity of choosing right over wrong in our own lives. Those who call upon him for help are often the poor, the marginalised and the oppressed, and their cry is a cry for justice. Knowing that God is a just God who will hear that cry and call the wicked to account is what gives hope to the downtrodden and the victims of injustice. It also serves as a deterrent to those who would do evil, for they know that they will answer to God for their actions.

Closing doxology (v. 21)

My mouth will speak in praise of the Lord.
Let every creature praise his holy name
for ever and ever.

Having started with praise, the psalm ends with a doxology. First the psalmist expresses a continuing personal determination to live a life characterised by praise, but then he summons the whole of the created world to join him in giving glory to God. Such an intention seems apposite in the light of all the truth that this psalm has unfolded for us, and it should be the ambition of every believer to live a praise-filled life: 'I will extol the Lord at all times; his praise will always be on my lips' (Psalm 34:1), and again, 'Praise the Lord, my soul; all my inmost being, praise his holy name' (103:1).

Here, then, is the background to the life of faith as it is normally experienced in the period of 'orientation', which, for most of us, is how things usually are. God is good and we are recipients of that goodness. Our lives are steady and secure. We see his greatness all around us, live securely under his sovereign rule, enjoy his faithful provision and know his protection. This is how God intends it to be, and it is what we come to expect—and perhaps here is where the danger lies. That which we happily receive at first as a gift soon becomes an expectation, and then a right, until we demand it and feel it is something we deserve. We can lose sight of knowing God for his own sake and become obsessed with his gifts. We no longer seek God for the joy of knowing him, but for what he can do for us or give to us. If we are truly to know God, we must distinguish between the blessing of God and the God of the blessings.

This is the background to the book of Job. Satan's accusation is that human beings, and Job in particular, never love God for his own sake but only for what they can get out of him. 'Does Job fear God for nothing?' is his taunt to the Almighty. 'Stretch out your hand and strike everything he has, and he will surely curse you to your face,' is his challenge (Job 1:9, 11). The Lord has confidence, though, in the reality of Job's faith, and allows him to be tested, knowing that he will come through the fiery trial not only with his faith intact but also purified like pure gold (23:10).

This is not unlike the experience of many of us as we seek to follow the Lord. Mostly, we live our lives with Psalm 145 as the background, and we are quietly thankful for God's goodness and grace. In particular, this will be so for those who are young in years or young in the faith. During this period, we seem to be blessed with an untroubled existence, as if we are specially protected as our faith takes root and we are established in God. Inevitably, though, because it is part of our spiritual formation, the day will come when our faith in God will be tested and we will be called upon to enter the valley of deep darkness. The phase of orientation will give way to a period of painful disorientation.

Questions will arise when we discover that life is not always as kind, fair or predictable as we imagined it would be or expected it should be. Painful events will call us to ask if God is really in control; we may wonder why a loving God allows bad things to happen to good people (and, equally troubling, why he allows good things to happen to bad people). For some, prayers will remain unanswered for no discernible reason; for others, the sense of God's close presence will be lost in a fog of uncertainty. 'Where are you, Lord?' becomes a common cry, and a song of lament forms on lips that previously had sung only songs of praise. Sadness may engulf us; joy may be lost. Darkness surrounds us. That which once was certain now seems less sure, and truths that once gripped us now appear to have been a lie. Spiritually we feel flat and lifeless, and the joy and assurance of others only adds to our pain. We wonder, 'Am I losing my faith?'

Is Psalm 145 an exaggeration, then? Does it paint a false picture? No, it isn't an exaggeration, and it is true—every word of it. God is great, he is loving, he is in control, he does provide for us, and he is just and worthy of praise. These things never change and are always true, but Psalm 145 does not give the whole picture. It deals with generalisations, things that are *normally* true. As Brueggemann points out, 'the text is dominated by the word *all*'.[11] At least 15 times the word 'all' is used. It makes comprehensive statements that apparently include everyone, but the bigger truth (both in scripture and in life) is that there are exceptions to these generalisations, and one day you or I may find that we are the exception to the rule. Something else is happening in our lives and we are walking a path that is different from the one described here. This will be unnerving and frightening, but we must remember that God is in it and we are still in the grip of grace. We are being taken into the depths so that we can know God more deeply, and, like Job, we shall eventually come forth refined like gold.

Psalm 145 is a psalm for a sunny day. Just as a picture taken in the height of summer reflects how the world often is at that time of year, this psalm shows how life with God looks most of the time. Indeed, many days are sunny and cloudless, but not all. Some days are grey and overcast, some days are stormy and wet, and a few days are cold and wintry. Whatever the season, though, God is with us, forming us and shaping us so that we can know him more fully, and our best learning often takes place when the season changes from summer to winter.

* * *

A letter from Mags, a good friend of mine and a mature believer, shows just how hard winter can be and how suddenly it can come upon us. She shares openly and honestly about her struggle to come to terms with a tragic loss. Her words reveal the reality of that struggle, but also show how much grace is given to those in the hard places of life.

5

Mags's story

11 November 2013

Dear Tony,

How are you? Trust that you are recovering from the latest round of jet lag!

It's Armistice Day today and on the TV news there are memorial services and clips from the day when the noise of battles was silenced and the noise of celebrations roared across the land. It's been a memorial day of sorts for me too today as I commemorate in my own heart three years ago today, when we got the news that Jenny had cancer. Ironic, really, that on the day when the world was commemorating peace, my own battles were just beginning.

As you know, having been with our mission in Asia for so many years, I'd missed most of Jenny's growing years, but, having returned home, I'd relished getting to know my only niece—my wonderful, amazing, beautiful niece. You would have loved her, Tony; she was funny and bright and loving and generous, and it was such a joy to come home and begin to get to know her. And then, this devastating, breath-snatching news.

My sister is a cancer nurse and that day she explained that Jenny didn't just have cancer, she had one of the rarest, most aggressive cancers known. And there was no cure, just a course of treatment that would, at the very best, extend her life for a few brief years. Jenny was 22; I had missed so much of her life. But she was not only my only niece; as I am a single woman, Jenny was like the daughter I never had and I loved her with every fibre of my being. This disease could not have her. So I began to pray, and I recruited friends from across the world to pray. A whole host of people prayed.

In the months that followed, as Jenny endured round after round of chemotherapy, radiotherapy, brachytherapy, and all the side-effects which accompanied these therapies, I prayed for healing. I appealed to the tender heart of the God I had known for over 40 years. I prayed through every round of therapy, every side effect, trusting that he would one day reveal with a flourish his healing hand—and Jenny would be freed from this cancer. I boldly claimed verses from the Psalms which spoke of God's power to heal, and asked others to pray them too. I brought God's word back to him, declaring the truth of God's word in Psalm 86:5: 'You are so good... so full of unfailing love for all who ask for your help.' And verse 15: 'You, O Lord, are a God of compassion and mercy... filled with unfailing love and faithfulness' (NLT). And my testimony echoed the psalmist's words in Psalm 88:13: 'I will keep on pleading day by day...' (NLT).

But nothing happened.

I sought out those who seemed to have the gift of faith and asked them to pray. As the only believer in my whole family, this was the one thing that I could do, that I could contribute to this awful situation—I could pray.

And Jenny got worse.

Month by month, she got worse. Every therapy failed. Nothing seemed to halt the onslaught, the ravages of this disease. But still I prayed; I believed God could heal my lovely Jenny. I fasted, first one day a week, then two days.

Other friends fasted with me. Nothing. Jenny's body seemed to be a playground for cancer as it spread into her organs, her spine, her lymph system; no part of her body was off limits to this insidious spread.

I stopped sharing prayer requests. It seemed that every time people prayed, she got worse. So I stopped asking people to pray. But I carried on quietly, hoping, trusting, for a miracle.

It took just over a year for the cancer to win the battle. In the last week of her life, Jenny's pain intensified beyond morphine's ability to keep up, and now my prayer became a pleading that God would take her. She had not been healed, but could he not now at least ease her passing? She was in pain, in distress, confused and so, so weary of it all. And still she lived on, and on.

On the night she was to die, I kissed her goodnight, whispered that I would see her in the morning and drove home to Mum's—just five minutes away. Mum was already in bed and so I crept up to my room and there I whispered my screams at God. Through gritted teeth I howled my rage at him. I pleaded for her release; I irrationally cajoled him with promises of fulfilling whatever sacrifice was necessary for me. I groaned my agony, and I threatened God; I threatened him that even though I could not stop believing in him, I would stop loving him. I would stop trusting his heart if he did not now have mercy on her.

At five minutes past midnight, as I lay exhausted on my bed, my nephew phoned to say that she had gone. A breath. A single tear. And she was gone.

And while my mother slept, unknowing, I sobbed my confusion and my grief.

Over the next days, both my thankfulness at her release

and my outrage at the wickedness of her death poured out of me, the walls of my tiny bedroom amazingly withstanding the onslaught of my whispered fury as I retreated there throughout those early days while my mother slept, exhausted from grief, in the next bedroom.

And then, the day before Jenny's funeral, I sat in the car in the driveway of our family home and, with my head on the steering wheel, I surrendered. The fight was all gone, the rage spent. I was depleted of all energy, and quietly and very calmly I spoke to God: 'There is no way out of this, there is only a way through it, and I choose to go through it with you. *But you have to be more.*'

And in the depths of my heart, I sensed a clear response, 'More I can do', and then very clearly, the words 'Mags, you have always trusted me as the God you know. Now I am asking you to trust me as the God you no longer recognise.'

Memories rushed in. Over many, many years I had come to know the Lord as good and kind and loving; he was my compassionate, tender God, the God of mercy and generous grace. Through hard times of deep disappointment, betrayal and dream-crushing circumstances, I had known and experienced his loving kindness. But after these battle-torn months of seemingly unanswered prayer, I had been faced with a God I no longer recognised. The clouds of grief and fear and pain had distorted his features; I could barely make out his outline through the veil of tears I lived with every day. The God I knew and loved had become a mystery to me. I no longer recognised him, but now, in the quietness of my car, on that last day of November 2010, a question rose in my heart: 'Who *are* you?' The answer was immediate and clear. In the very depths of my soul I heard him say, 'I am your Emmanuel; I am *with* you; I AM with you.'

And finally, peace. No healing, no resurrection, no miracle —except this miracle of peace. He had broken through with the promise of his presence, and it was enough. And it has been enough over these past three tear-laden years.

I don't know if you knew it, but Jenny was a medal-winning runner, a sprinter. Some months after Jenny's death, I came across this quote by Eric Liddell, another runner, written from the Japanese prison camp where he was interned, and it resonated at some deep level in me: 'Circumstances may appear to wreck our lives and God's plans, but God is not helpless among the ruins.'

Tony, one thing I am learning through all of this, amazingly, is that my peace rests in the mystery of who God is; I know he is good—but there is mystery in how he demonstrates that goodness. These past days of remembering have been harder days, but underneath the grief is a peace that really does pass understanding—and reaches out to touch the face of mystery.

Love and blessings,
Mags

6

Psalm 130:
The depths of failure

From the stability and peace of a period of 'orientation' described in Psalm 145, we turn now to a psalm that reflects the experience of disorientation, the kind that is brought about by human failure—in particular, the failure that we call sin.

The Bible uses many words to describe sin, such as 'transgression', 'iniquity' and 'trespass', but the most common idea behind the word in both Testaments is 'to miss the mark'—a failure to hit the target. It suggests an archer taking aim, only to find that the shot has either fallen short or gone wide of the mark. When we sin, we fall short of God's standards and fail to live up to his ideal, either doing what we should not do, or not doing what we should do. Sometimes the sin may be intentional, at other times it may be accidental, but either way we fail to make the grade. According to the apostle Paul, this is a universal condition, 'for all have sinned and fall short of the glory of God' (Romans 3:23).

Failure has many other expressions, and God sometimes uses our failures to show us our need of him. Most of us do our best to avoid failure because it is a painful and humbling experience. Some of us work hard to make sure we never fail, being driven by perfectionist tendencies that compel us to succeed at everything we do. Others play safe, avoiding any challenge that we fear we may not be able to meet, because we are so afraid of failure. Sooner or later, though, all of us will experience failure in some form and will have to come to terms with the reality that we are not perfect. We fail as parents; we fail as lovers; we fail as friends. We fail to achieve our ambitions; we fail to be the people we want to be; we fail to keep our word; we fail to break the habits that bind us. The question is: where will we go with our failure? How will we handle our imperfections?

We are not sure who wrote Psalm 130 or the nature of the particular sins that gave rise to it, but we do know that it stems from a deep experience of failure before God. It is one of seven 'penitential psalms', which all deal with the issue of personal failure, the others being Psalms 6, 32, 38, 51, 102 and 143. The anonymity of the prayer and the lack of specific detail mean that its message has a timeless quality. It can speak helpfully to anyone, at any time, dealing with any form of failure. Interestingly, it is also one of the 15 'songs of ascents' in the book of Psalms, psalms that were sung by pilgrims as they made their way to Jerusalem. Sometimes these songs would be sung on the temple steps as the walkers drew near to God, each step indicating an upward movement. Psalm 130 reminds us, though, that in the spiritual life the way up often leads downwards first. Only when we are willing to acknowledge our sin and failure can we know God's forgiveness, and only then can we draw near to him with confidence. So it is that this little psalm begins in the depths but ends on the heights.

As we read the psalm, we will trace the journey made by its writer as he (assuming the author is a man) works his way through the pain of failure in the context of his relationship with God and the community of faith. The structure of the psalm suggests four steps or phases in the process of lament and recovery.

Step 1: He cries to God (vv. 1–2)

> *A song of ascents.*
> *Out of the depths I cry to you, O Lord;*
> *Lord, hear my voice.*
> *Let your ears be attentive*
> *to my cry for mercy.*

Whatever has happened in his life, the psalmist finds himself in a deep place. The language he uses ('out of the depths') is suggestive of being overwhelmed by feelings and emotions, a bit like drowning in a vast ocean. This metaphor is common in the Psalms and elsewhere, and aptly portrays the sense of disorientation that we sometimes experience (Psalm 69:1–2, 14–15; 93:3–4; 124:4–5; Jonah 2:3; Exodus 15:5). James W. Sire comments:

> *For the psalmist 'the deep', the sea or the ocean, is a primal force of chaos; God has created and ordered it, but it still threatens to undo humankind. When the psalmist calls from the depths, then, he is calling from a place of danger with a fear of being overwhelmed, in particular from the chaos of the sins that encompass him.*[12]

The consequences of sin are indeed chaotic. Sin creates a mess in our personal life and often also in the lives of others. Its negative effects have a way of spreading like poisonous tendrils and drawing in those around us. Sin causes a traumatic emotional response within us. We feel the anguish of guilt, the pain of shame, the relentless throb of remorse. We may become bitter and twisted, blaming others, refusing to forgive and being overwhelmed by self-pity. Worst of all, though, sin separates us from God, alienates us from our source of peace and joy, and cuts us off from the one who alone can help us. No wonder the Bible describes sin as a disease, for it creates a serious dis-ease within us. It can take a toll on our health and physical well-being and can affect us mentally, especially when it is hidden or unacknowledged (Psalm 32:3–4; 38:1–8).

Happily for the psalmist, he chooses not to stay in his sin or to seek a self-help solution for his pain. He turns instinctively to God for help, remembering, no doubt, that 'the Lord is gracious and compassionate, slow to anger and rich in love' (Psalm 145:8). He knows that despite his failure, guilt and shame, he can turn to God in his need because 'the Lord is near to all who call on him, to all who call on him in truth' (v. 18). This cry for help, this cry of a drowning man, is directed towards God because the psalmist knows deep within himself that God is merciful. If he knew this before in his head, now he will learn it in his heart.

The kind of brokenness and humility that failure brings can be a stepping stone to a deeper relationship with God. Once we stop pretending, covering up, making excuses, rationalising and so on, we are free to be real with ourselves and before God. God knows the worst about us and loves us just the same. This truth sets us free to drop our masks and stop our play-acting. It is painful to be stripped of all self-righteousness but it has to happen if we are to encounter God in a real way.

Step 2: He believes in God (vv. 3–4)

If you, O Lord, kept a record of sins,
O Lord, who could stand?
But with you there is forgiveness;
therefore you are feared.

These days, organisations hold all kinds of records about us—medical records, dental records, phone records, bank details, credit card transactions and so on. If I use my loyalty card in the coffee shop, the firm knows about it and will ask me for feedback online; if I make a transaction on Amazon, I will soon receive an email recommending other similar products. We may think our lives are private but they are not. Our movements can be tracked from our phones, and our whereabouts noted on CCTV.

If we think we can hide our sin from God, we are even more mistaken. He knows the law because he gave it. He sees everything and knows when we transgress. He discerns our innermost thoughts and is aware of our sinful attitudes. He weighs our actions and examines our motivations, and nothing escapes his notice. What is more, he never forgets. So what if God were to keep a record of our sin, of my sin?

Well, if he did, we would stand before him guilty and for ever condemned. The way into his presence would for ever be closed to us. That's why, when we read Psalm 24:3–4, we should be disturbed: 'Who may ascend the hill of the Lord? Who may stand in his holy place? He who has clean hands and a pure heart, who does not lift up his soul to an idol or swear by what is false.' How many of us would qualify on this basis? None, but the good news is that God does not keep a record of our sin. That was the sweet discovery that the psalmist made as he cried out to God for mercy. In the distress of his failure, he stumbled across an amazing truth that would change his life and the lives of others.

Here it is: 'But with you there is forgiveness' (Psalm 130:4). Don't underestimate the significance of the word 'but' in this sentence. It marks a contrast and highlights a difference. It could have been that God kept a record of my sin... *but* that is not the case. Why? Because in the heart of God there is the desire to forgive, to wash us clean and take away our sin and its stain. This is the truth that the psalmist took hold of as he turned back to God—or, perhaps more correctly, this was the truth that took hold of him as he cried out for forgiveness. It was a truth implicit in the sacrificial system of the Old Testament and was revealed in part by God's self-disclosure to Moses (Exodus 34:6–7): God is a forgiving God. Wilcock comments, 'The New Testament has told us how a God who hates sin can forgive it. The psalmist has grasped the fact, though he perceives less of the method than we do, knowing the Old Testament sacrifices but not yet the sacrifice of Calvary.'[13]

Forgiveness originates with God. He is under no obligation to forgive, and we have no leverage to make him do so. It is his free and gracious act, and he does so on the basis of Christ's atoning death at Calvary: 'In him we have redemption through his blood, the forgiveness of sins, in accordance with the riches of God's grace' (Ephesians 1:7). Forgiveness implies the healing of a broken relationship, a reconciliation of those who were estranged, a recovery of friendship and intimacy, a new beginning. When we receive it, it is complete, total and for ever. The record is annulled and will never be brought up again. 'He forgave us all our sins, having cancelled the written code, with its regulations, that was against us and that stood opposed to us; he took it away, nailing it to the cross' (Colossians 2:13–14). The law can no longer condemn us (Romans 8:1).

The immediate impact of such grace is seen in a new resolve to serve God and a new desire to obey his law. This seems to be the meaning of the expression 'therefore you are feared' in Psalm 130:4. A deep lesson has been learned in the experience of failure. To be the recipient of such grace causes a deep respect for God to be born in the psalmist's heart and a new humility in his disposition. He does not want to walk that way again; he has learned his lesson well. From now on, a different motivation fills his heart. He has been chastened, humbled, changed. As an updated translation puts it, 'But with you there is forgiveness, so that we can, with reverence, serve you' (NIV 2011).

Step 3: He waits for God

> *I wait for the Lord, my soul waits,*
> *and in his word I put my hope.*
> *My soul waits for the Lord*
> *more than watchmen wait for the morning,*
> *more than watchmen wait for the morning.*

The psalmist seems now to enter a period of waiting, but waiting for what? It feels to him as if he is like a watchman guarding the city overnight and waiting eagerly for the dawn, but the night drags on and it seems as if morning will never come. Will the sun ever rise again? The intensity of this waiting time is communicated by the way the phrase 'more than watchmen wait for the morning' is repeated. The anguish comes across in that the psalmist regards his own waiting as 'more than' that of the watchmen, perhaps because they know exactly when their shift will end, while he has no idea when his own waiting will be over.

Waiting is a common experience of people in a period of spiritual disorientation. It seems to be part of the agenda that God has for us, for we are usually impatient and anxious to move forward before the deep work in our souls is really finished. We are not really very patient, but God is never in a hurry and he will take all the time he needs to make sure that we have grasped the lessons he wants to teach us before allowing us to move on. In such periods of waiting, our hope has to be firmly placed in God's word—either a scriptural promise or something he has said to us personally. Again, we are brought back to the foundational truths of Psalm 145 and the faithfulness of God: 'The Lord is faithful to all his promises and loving toward all he has made' (v. 13b). Times of waiting are times when we can anchor our souls in the truth of God's word and his faithfulness in bringing it to pass at the right time. God will not be hurried or cajoled into acting according to our timetable. Like Habakkuk, we may cry out 'How long?' but the answer will always be the same: 'For the revelation awaits an appointed time; it speaks of the end and will not prove false. Though it linger, wait for it; it will certainly come and will not delay' (Habakkuk 2:3).

Isn't forgiveness immediate, though? For what could the psalmist be waiting? It may be oversimplifying things to say he is waiting for daybreak, but in reality he is. He is waiting for the truth to dawn upon his soul and take full possession of him. Yes, forgiveness as far as God is concerned is immediate and complete, the moment we confess our sin to him, but the experience of being forgiven may take a little while longer to dawn upon us.

In the first place, it can be hard to believe that we are forgiven. It can seem too easy. We may feel we have to make atonement ourselves or that we don't deserve to be let off so quickly, so painlessly. We may struggle with the memories of what happened, and guilt and shame can be difficult to dislodge from our hearts, even when our heads tell us we are forgiven. Furthermore, we may find it hard to forgive ourselves even though we know that God has forgiven us. We may want to keep blaming ourselves and to punish ourselves for being so foolish or careless or thoughtless. Remorse can grip our souls like a vice and may be hard to shift. It takes time for the liberating truth of God's forgiving word to do its complete work. Forgiveness is akin to healing, and healing takes time.

In addition, we may have to wait for others to be ready to forgive us. If we have hurt others by our sinfulness, we can be forgiven by God but we will perhaps know full release only when we hear those we have hurt saying that they too forgive us. Relationships can remain strained for a long time, and reconciliation is never easy; indeed, it isn't always possible and, in some cases, may not be right. Similarly, we may need time and space so that we are ready to forgive those who have hurt us. These things cannot be rushed, and we require God's ongoing work in our hearts.

Finally, because there are consequences to our sin, it can take time for those consequences to be worked through. Sometimes we will have to learn to live with the fruits of our actions, which will be a constant reminder to us of past mistakes. This is why we need to be anchored firmly to God's word. Satan is the accuser and he loves nothing better than to undermine our confidence in God by drawing our attention to our sin. Only when we are fully convinced that our sins have been forgiven and will be remembered no more can we silence his condemning words.

Step 4: He speaks of God (vv. 7–8)

O Israel, put your hope in the Lord,
for with the Lord is unfailing love
and with him is full redemption.
He himself will redeem Israel
from all their sins.

The final verses of Psalm 130 see the psalmist, having passed through his period of disorientation, now in the place of reorientation where he has a testimony to share and wisdom to communicate to others. This is one of the benefits of difficult times. They do not last for ever and they result in changed behaviour and a deeper grasp of familiar truth. In other words, they are transformative.

Perhaps there has been a time gap between verses 6 and 7. Certainly the psalmist now speaks with greater confidence about a God he knows and an experience he understands. His failure seems to be in the past, and he is now able to share with authority the things he has learned. Kidner writes, 'There is a steady climb towards assurance, and at the end there is encouragement for the many from the experience of the one... The singer is now liberated from himself to turn to his people and hold out hopes that are far from tentative.'[14]

The psalmist's exhortation of his own people reflects the revelation that has come to him during his crisis, and, in urging his friends to put their hope in the Lord, he is asking them to take confidence in who God is. He speaks with authority and assurance because he speaks from his own experience. He has fallen, but he has fallen into grace and thereby discovered the reality of God's love and saving power. First, he points to God's unfailing love. God's love is a covenant-keeping love; it is steadfast and sure, and will never fail. What this means is that God will never stop loving us, no matter how we have failed or however many times we have fallen. He will never let go of us, and we can always turn back to him. We may be faithless, but he will always be faithful (2 Timothy 2:13).

Second, the psalmist directs his listeners to the salvation that is available to them in God: 'with him is full redemption' (v. 7). Israel always regarded the great rescue act that was the exodus from Egypt as an act of redemption, and thought of God as their redeemer (Exodus 15:13; Psalm 25:22; 26:11; Isaiah 44:6, 24; 60:16; 63:16). He is the one who can lift them out of their distress and bring them up from the depths. He can break the chains of sin and liberate them from guilt and shame. This he can do for individuals, and this he can do for the nation. He urges them to put their hope, their faith, in this powerful, saving God.

The final sentence of the psalm not only attributes redemption to the action of God alone, but also looks forward to the day when he will bring about a perfect redemption through the saving work of his Son: 'He *himself* will redeem Israel from all their sins' (v. 8, emphasis added). At the cross, God acted in Christ to provide a free and full forgiveness for the whole world. God was in Christ reconciling the world to himself (2 Corinthians 5:19). That is why the psalmist's words can speak to us today. His invitation is not just for Israel but for people of all nations at all times. They are words for you and me today as we read them in this present moment. If we have fallen or failed, redemption is freely available. We too can know this full and complete forgiveness. By God's grace we can be lifted from the depths to the heights.

When Avril's marriage collapsed, she felt a failure and found herself cast into a deep place like that described in Psalm 130. She would face a long, hard struggle for spiritual survival in which forgiveness would play a key part and would take a long time to come to pass.

7

Avril's story

The first verse of Psalm 130 in THE MESSAGE says, 'Help, God—the bottom has fallen out of my life!' This is a fairly accurate description of how I felt when my marriage of 20 years collapsed around me in 2000. When I saw the TV footage of the earthquake and tsunami in Japan in 2011, I related my own feelings to the total devastation that was the result, and the grief and despair felt by those people of Japan.

When I first found out that my husband had fallen in love with someone else and, eventually, that he wanted a divorce, I felt as though I had been thrown into a very deep place, a place that was overwhelming me and one I would never come out of. All I could think was that this didn't happen to someone like me. We were a happy family (or so I thought), active in our church, so why would God allow it?

In Psalm 130, the psalmist is calling out to God from a place where he (or she) feels overwhelmed by the chaos that sin has created. I remember crying and sobbing so hard, it felt almost as though the sobs came from the pit of my stomach and as if my whole body was being turned inside out. I felt a mixture of despair, confusion, shame, fear and isolation from God. I would cry out to God to rescue me: 'Listen hard! Open your ears! Listen to my cries for mercy' (v. 1). At the time, I could not 'feel' God, but one thing I did know was that he was the only one I could turn to.

The years that followed could only be described as 'survival'. I felt a failure because my marriage had broken down, but God was with me through it all, in every tiny faltering step I made. I was given a 'picture' at church one Sunday evening of a dove with a broken wing that couldn't fly but one day would be mended and fly again. I was that dove. A few days afterwards, I looked out of my bedroom window and, amazingly, saw two white doves sitting on the pavement opposite my house. As I watched, they turned towards me, then both flew away. I felt as if God was saying to me that he knew all about my situation and that I would one day fly again.

The experience of our divorce badly scarred both my daughters, who were 12 and 14 at the time. My one prayer at the outset of this horrendous time was that God would keep and guard my daughters, and I can now give God all the praise and thanks for what he has done for them.

For more than ten years I felt as if I was on a steep upward climb, and at times I wondered whether God had forgotten me. However, I can now see that the brokenness and depths of despair I was experiencing had, in fact, become stepping stones to a deeper and more meaningful relationship with God. I had no choice but to lean on God and his promises and to trust him day by day: 'I pray to God—my life a prayer—and wait for what he'll say and do' (v. 5).

At the end of September 2010, my church was conducting a course known as the *Freedom in Christ* course, which I attended. One session concentrated on the subject of forgiveness. We were encouraged to sit and ask God to reveal any unforgiveness in our hearts. My thoughts naturally turned to my marriage breakdown. I had always known I must forgive all the hurts and injustices directed at me, and had striven to do this with the help and support of Christian friends. I therefore felt confused about what God was asking of me.

The answer came through a conversation with my youngest daughter. She had been praying and felt God telling her that I must be reconciled to her dad. For many reasons, too many to mention, this was a seemingly unbelievable and impossible scenario. However, God showed me very clearly that it was not just forgiveness he required of me, but also reconciliation.

What ensued were many days of earnestly seeking and waiting on God, together with feelings of confusion, fear and disbelief. I contacted my ex-husband (who had now remarried) and asked if I could meet up with him and his wife. The days and weeks leading up to this meeting were some of the most excruciating, yet amazing, of my Christian experience. God gave me a picture of a baby in a birth canal, with only one way to go—forwards, no way back. The passage was tight and narrow and painful for the mother, but the experience was essential in order to bring birth to the baby. I desperately wanted to call friends to help me through, but each time God clearly said, 'No, this is just you and me. I don't want you to hear any voice other than mine.' I remember, when I was giving birth to my two daughters, using the words 'I can't do this!' and these were words I cried out on many occasions during the weeks before meeting my ex-husband. All I could do was 'watch and wait' for God to bring about a 'birth': 'My life's on the line before God, my Lord, waiting and watching till morning' (v. 6).

I did meet with my ex-husband and his wife, and God's amazing power within me enabled me to tell my ex-husband that I did not hold him to account for anything: I knew it was God's will for us to be reconciled and thereby freed to be the people he wanted us to be. I prayed with them that God would bless them in their marriage and set them free to do his will.

God revealed to me that Satan had blinded me to the stronghold he had on my life. I had come to accept the continual stronghold of conflict with my ex-husband, a pattern of thought and behaviour that I always felt could never change. I was locked in a 'deep darkness', like a prison of bitterness and regret. God gave me the strength I needed to forgive, let go and be reconciled. The picture of the dove became a reality: God was showing me how I would fly and be free again, the darkness giving way to light.

I learnt that I needed to rebuke Satan's lies, which allow negative thoughts into our hearts. I am precious and honoured in God's sight, his beloved child, not a weakling or a failure. God gives and we receive; God speaks and we listen and are changed: 'O Israel, wait and watch for God—with God's arrival comes love, with God's arrival comes generous redemption' (v. 7).

God has done, and is still doing, a loving and restoring work in my life. My prayer is that I will continue to live in the truth of the freedom that God has given to me and my family.

8

Psalm 42 and 43:
The depths of despair

I have a vivid memory from my teenage years of my father suffering a severe bout of depression. He had lost his job and fallen into a pit of despair, what we would call today a 'reactive depression'. He would sit for long hours staring into space, saying nothing, locked into dark introspection and feeling that the world was against him. We felt powerless to help him. Fortunately, after a spell in hospital he recovered and, after several months, returned to normal, but I will never forget the trauma of those days in our family.

It is said that one in four people in Britain will have an episode of mental illness at some point in their life. Depression is defined by the World Health Organisation as 'a common mental disorder, characterised by sadness, loss of interest or pleasure, feelings of guilt or low self-worth, disturbed sleep or appetite, feelings of tiredness, and poor concentration'.[15] All of us know what it is to have days when we feel blue, and many of us will have experienced mild depression (often brought on by external negative factors, the stress and strains of life and different kinds of loss that we experience), which usually leaves us after a while. Some, though, may experience more long-term, 'chronic' depression, which is usually biological in origin, caused by chemical imbalance in the brain.

In this pair of psalms (which really belong together as

one, since they share a common theme and have a common refrain) we meet a musician who is in the depths of despair. Psalm 42 is described as a 'maskil', and, although we do not understand all the musical terms used in the Psalms, this one seems to mean a song of instruction. Perhaps the thought is that even in the deepest sorrow the soul can still turn towards God. It is attributed to the sons of Korah, a guild of musicians responsible for the temple worship. In all probability, the writer was one of their number. He speaks about leading others in worship (42:4) and of playing the harp (43:4). He is a person of strong faith, for God is his Rock (42:9), his stronghold (43:2), his Saviour (v. 5) and, indeed, the source of his life (42:8). And yet he is depressed.

Some Christians think that a believer should never be depressed, but these psalms would suggest otherwise. We are human, we have feelings, and sometimes we will get depressed. The psalmist shows many of the classic symptoms of depression. He is downcast (42:5), which means that his mood is low; he is lacking in joy and feeling pessimistic. He is also disturbed within—full of anxious and troubled thoughts, perhaps agitated and restless, lacking in the peace that would normally characterise his life, and probably not sleeping well. He is tearful and prone to weeping, and has lost his appetite for food (v. 3). He is cheerless and sad, full of grief, moping around with no enthusiasm, and lacking in energy. He feels oppressed, as if people are against him (v. 9), and over-whelmed by life (v. 7). All this emotional pain is affecting him physically, too. It may be psychosomatic, but his whole body aches and the physical pain is real (v. 10).

What has caused such despair? We can only surmise, but it seems that for some reason this godly musician has been cut off from the temple that he loves and the role he delights to play there. His depression is, in all likelihood, caused by grief, a typical response to significant losses or reversals of fortune. Kidner suggests that he is a temple singer who has been exiled in the north of the country, away from his normal surroundings, job and friends.[16] Other scholars suggest that he is one of those who has experienced the downfall of Jerusalem and the destruction of the temple, and is now in exile in Babylon. This traumatic loss has thrown him into the most profound turmoil, emotionally and spiritually.

The kind of suffering described here could also be seen as 'spiritual depression', in that the loss experienced would raise deep questions for someone of faith. Beyond the trauma of the devastating defeat and cruel destruction that Israel suffered at the hands of the Babylonians, for this man of faith there was an equal spiritual trauma. How could God allow such a thing to happen? How could worship ever be the same again? Why had God forsaken and abandoned his people? These questions are typical of lament psalms and they are embedded in these beautifully crafted but poignant words. At heart, it is the psalmist's relationship with God that has been destabilised, and he finds himself now in a painful period of disorientation.

We may indeed wonder why God allows such times of despair to come upon us. Rightly understood, though, these periods can become opportunities for significant learning and a rethinking of our faith, resulting in a deeper relationship with God and a transformed self. If we are willing to be honest before God, as the psalmist is here, opening ourselves up to what he may have to teach us, we can find that even the darkness of depression can serve the purpose of God.

There is a definite structure uniting the two psalms, and the chorus running through them reminds us that this song would originally have been composed by the musician as a way of expressing his feelings and coming to terms with his despair. It is therefore instructive for us, showing how to deal with our own periods of grief, loss and disappointment.

The basic structure looks like this:

42:1–4   'I feel dry'
42:5   The chorus: 'Why are you downcast?'
42:6–10 'I feel overwhelmed'
42:11   The chorus: 'Why are you downcast?'
43:1–4   'I feel abandoned'
43:5   The chorus: 'Why are you downcast?'

We can see immediately that the writer is honestly expressing his distress, but, each time, he counters his despair with a personal pep talk. An inner dialogue is taking place, as well as a conversation with God and with the people listening to the song. There is ebb and flow as dark emotions are challenged by the light of God's truth. It is not an easy battle to win, and even at the end of the psalm we do not know for certain if the writer has conquered his despair once and for all. This biblical realism is important, though, for depressed people are too often told, 'Pull yourself together' or 'Snap out of it', when in reality it is rarely that simple. Yet we do not need to be prisoners to dark thoughts for ever, and these psalms give us hope that we can, and will, find a way through to normality again.

I feel dry (42:1–4)

As the deer pants for streams of water,
so my soul pants for you, O God.

My soul thirsts for God, for the living God.
When can I go and meet with God?
My tears have been my food
day and night,
while men say to me all day long,
'Where is your God?'
These things I remember
as I pour out my soul:
how I used to go with the multitude,
leading the procession to the house of God
with shouts of joy and thanksgiving
among the festive throng.

The psalm begins with a moving expression of thirst for God. This godly musician still longs for God but his need cannot be easily be satisfied, and is therefore itself an agony. It is the thirst of a deer being chased by hunters, with no time to stop and drink, for whom the thirst has become a torture. For the psalmist, the soul-agonising question is 'When can I go and meet with God?' (v. 2). In this foreign land, where is God to be found when we can no longer worship in the temple?

The taunts of his enemies exacerbate his pain, for they know how to hit where it hurts most. 'Where is your God?' they ask, and he has no answer, for it seems that the God of Israel has been defeated. Further, his own sweet memories have a bitter taste. He remembers well the happier days when he led the multitudes in temple worship, but now that is a distant memory and those days are gone, probably for ever. 'I used to…' (v. 4) is a very sad expression and sums up his despair and disappointment as the tears flow again. Here is a leader who has lost his way.

The chorus (v. 5)

Why are you downcast, O my soul?
Why so disturbed within me?
Put your hope in God,
for I will yet praise him,
my Saviour and my God.

The chorus is, without doubt, the central part of the psalm, representing the way the writer calls on his spiritual reserves to wrestle with his despair. The fact that it is repeated three times suggests that it is spoken with greater feeling each time as he seeks to apply the truth to his life. There is no magic formula that we can use to cast off depression, but we can determine to work against being overwhelmed by negative thoughts or painful emotions; we can bring the truth of God to bear on our circumstances and seek liberation from the clouds that would envelop us. This point is emphasised by Dr Martyn Lloyd-Jones in his classic book on the subject of spiritual depression. He wisely observes that, at such times, 'We must talk to ourselves, instead of allowing "ourselves" to talk to us. Most of your unhappiness in life is due to the fact that you are listening to yourself instead of talking to yourself.'[17]

As we ponder the psalmist's words here, we can identify four important aspects of this spiritual fightback.

• **Be honest:** the writer does not pretend that things are 'OK' or 'fine' when they are not. He identifies his emotional state candidly as being 'downcast' and 'disturbed'. Such candour is the gift of the psalms of lament, which show us that true prayer can mean getting things off our chest and expressing our feelings openly before God. He does not object to it, and neither should we be afraid of such self-disclosure; it is part of finding healing and release.

- **Ask questions:** the psalmist interrogates himself, seeking to get to the root of the matter and understand the source of his despair. In asking 'Why?' he is speaking to himself, to his own soul. Honest self-examination can be really helpful in tracing our thought patterns, for it is often faulty thinking that leads to negative emotions. One of the things that can happen during a time of disorientation is that we are made aware of any such faulty thinking, especially our inadequate theology. We may not even realise that our thinking is askew unless something happens to make us reconsider our beliefs. So, if the psalmist believes that Judah's defeat by the Babylonians means that God himself is defeated, then certainly it is cause for despair—but is that truly the case, or is there another explanation for what has happened? That is what the psalmist must ponder.

- **Have faith:** isn't it surprising how often we know the answer to our own questions? If only we will stop and listen to our hearts, the answer is right there within us. After questioning himself, the psalmist now exhorts himself with what he knows deep within to be the best response: he must hope in God. To hope in God is to believe that ultimately God will prove himself to be God, that his promises will come to pass and his word will show itself to be true. It is to believe that his actions are just, fair and loving, even when we don't understand them. It is to believe that things will work out in the end, even if there seems no possibility of that happening in the present. But this requires faith, and faith is the opposite of sight (2 Corinthians 5:7; Hebrews 11:1). Faith is something we choose to exercise. It is never blind, because it is faith in

God and finds its strength from who he is and what we know him to be. Hebrews 11 gives a wonderful account of men and women who chose to walk by faith despite contrary circumstances that would have caused them to doubt. The psalmist has to make this choice in the loneliness and isolation of exile, so he speaks the words of faith—'for I will yet praise him'—refusing to give way to hopelessness, choosing to believe that the day will come when his voice will be lifted up once more in worship to God (see 2 Corinthians 4:13).

- **Lean hard:** faith must have an object. We must know who we believe, and the psalmist is in no doubt where his trust lies. It is in 'my Saviour and my God'. The use of the personal word 'my' suggests an intimate relationship with God, with a history behind it and a deep heart connection. Such a relationship may well be tested and shaken to the core, but it will survive because it is God who holds the believer, not the other way round. His covenant faithfulness is what we rest upon. He is our rock, our stronghold, the God of our life. We can lay the full weight of our hopes upon him, and we will not be disappointed.

I feel overwhelmed (vv. 6–10)

My soul is downcast within me;
therefore I will remember you
from the land of the Jordan,
the heights of Hermon—from Mount Mizar.
Deep calls to deep
in the roar of your waterfalls;
all your waves and breakers
have swept over me.

> *By day the Lord directs his love,*
> *at night his song is with me—*
> *a prayer to the God of my life.*
> *I say to God my Rock,*
> *'Why have you forgotten me?*
> *Why must I go about mourning,*
> *oppressed by the enemy?'*
> *My bones suffer mortal agony*
> *as my foes taunt me,*
> *saying to me all day long,*
> *'Where is your God?'*

The first singing of the chorus lays a marker down, but the battle is not yet won. Waves of despair sweep over the psalmist's soul and soon he is engulfed again. He remembers fondly his homeland—the Jordan river, the majesty of Hermon, the beauty of Mount Mizar—but homesickness grips him and his soul is flooded with sadness. His soul is battered by negativity just as the coast is battered by stormy waves and breakers, smashing at his resolve, eroding his faith (vv. 6–7). Yet even then, there is a still small voice reminding him of God's love. In the middle of the night, when sleep has deserted him, a song rises from somewhere in his heart to God, and he knows that God is doing something in his life, inviting him to a deeper level of faith and trust, for 'deep calls to deep'.

Then again the doubts return. Once more he speaks honestly to his God: 'Why have you forgotten me?' It isn't true that God has forgotten him, of course, but it feels true, especially when he is being taunted and is in pain, and grief overcomes him (vv. 9–10). Grief is like that, isn't it, coming at us in waves, returning to disturb us just when we thought we were through it? And with the grief comes pain, and with the pain, anger and the need to blame someone, especially God.

The chorus repeated (v. 11)

Why are you downcast, O my soul?
Why so disturbed within me?
Put your hope in God,
for I will yet praise him,
my Saviour and my God.

We have to admire the singer's spiritual resolve: although he is battered and bruised, he refuses to give up the fight. Once more he goes through his survival pattern: honesty, self-reflection, the choice to believe, then leaning hard on God and entrusting himself to his faithfulness. That is all he can do, but strength returns and hope is fired again.

I feel abandoned (43:1–4)

Vindicate me, O God,
and plead my cause against an ungodly nation;
rescue me from deceitful and wicked men.
You are God my stronghold.
Why have you rejected me?
Why must I go about mourning,
oppressed by the enemy?
Send forth your light and your truth,
let them guide me;
let them bring me to your holy mountain,
to the place where you dwell.
Then I will go to the altar of God,
to God, my joy and my delight.

I will praise you with the harp,
O God, my God.

If the psalmist will not give in, neither will his opponent. It feels like a boxing match, and another round begins. Now his feeling has turned to rejection, a sense of being abandoned by God. To be forgotten is one thing; to be abandoned is altogether more painful. He needs God to stand up for him, to protect him from his enemies, to vindicate him in front of those who accuse him of believing in vain. Why must the torment continue? Why doesn't God intervene (vv. 1–2)?

Yet he is not abandoned, and once again the grace of God seeks him out. A prayer for light and truth forms in his heart, for he knows that this is what he needs if he is ever to rediscover his place with God. Only a fresh revelation from God will suffice; only a God-given understanding will see him through (v. 3). Faith is rising now, and a picture forms in his mind. He can see himself before the altar, worshipping God with joy and delight, leading others again in happy celebration of their Lord (v. 4). It is still future, but faith lives in the future, and he knows that it will soon become the present.

The chorus repeated again (v. 5)

Why are you downcast, O my soul?
Why so disturbed within me?
Put your hope in God,
for I will yet praise him,
my Saviour and my God.

For a final time the singer turns to his cherished refrain, but this time with greater confidence than before. Light is dawning, the fog is lifting, and he is finding his way home again. He is still honest but the words 'downcast' and 'disturbed' have lost their sting; they are defeated. He has examined his soul and begun to make adjustments to his thinking. Perhaps God has not abandoned his people after all. Maybe he is working out his purposes even in and through the disaster of defeat and exile. Praise is returning to the psalmist's lips again and joy is in his heart. There is hope, the confident expectation of good to come—and of course he is leaning more fully than ever before on his Saviour and God, for he has been brought to a new place of both dependency and intimacy.

The journey of the psalmist in Psalms 42 and 43 is a good example of both the process of lament and the experience of disorientation. God will sometimes allow events to destabilise us so that we can examine the foundations of our faith and thereby find a firmer footing. It may be disturbing to think that God is behind a period of despair and depression, but that seems to be the implication in 42:7, where it says, 'All *your* waves and breakers have swept over me' (emphasis added). If we have a faulty understanding of God, it needs to be exposed and corrected so that we may grow stronger in faith. This is one of the gifts of the valley experience.

We cannot say for certain how or when the exiled singer was liberated totally from his depression, but I think we are safe to assume that he was, and also that he learned some precious lessons. Indeed, one of the benefits was that he could write a song of such beauty and truth, which would continue to help and guide people down the centuries. This mature faith does not come easily; it is the result of the painful process of spiritual formation.

I think we can also see how his questions may have been answered by God.

- When can I go and meet with God? (42:2). 'Now!' Any time, any place, because God is everywhere, not limited to Jerusalem. We take this truth for granted in our new covenant days, but it was a radically new thought for Israel, which took shape only through the questioning that went on during the exile.
- Why have you forgotten me? (42:9). 'I haven't and I never will.' It may feel as if God is neglecting us, but he never will, despite our feelings. Difficult circumstances do not equate to withdrawal of his love or care. Indeed, as the apostle Paul would joyfully proclaim, nothing can separate us from the love of God in Christ Jesus (Romans 8:37–39).
- Why have you rejected me? (43:2). 'I couldn't and I wouldn't.' The grip of God's covenant love is too strong for him ever to abandon us, and nothing we can ever do will cause him to stop loving us. We are safe and secure in his love. He will never leave us or forsake us (Hebrews 13:5).

These are precious truths and they came to light in the midst of the darkness that was the exile. God had not been defeated: Israel learned to sing the Lord's song again, even in a foreign land (Psalm 137:4), and they returned from Babylon stronger and purer in faith than when they left Jerusalem. If our singer was one of those who returned, we can picture him taking his place in worship at the rebuilt temple with a renewed faith and deeper joy than ever before. It is only by walking through our own valleys that we too will be gripped by the truth of God's invincible love; it may require a valley experience, but we will come through the darkness deeper in faith and closer to God than we were.

* * *

Depression is a real issue, even for Christians and even for leaders. Psalms 42 and 43 do not promise easy answers or a quick way through, but they do remind us that there is hope. Keep the psalmist's words in your mind as you read the story of one Australian church leader who has also battled with depression.

9

Rick's story

I was sitting in a seminar about depression when it occurred to me that what the speaker, Archibald Hart, was describing was precisely what I had been experiencing for some months. This was an unexpected and significant realisation for me. I had known something was wrong but it needed someone skilled to connect the dots for me. It was like a light coming on.

Until then, I'd had some pretty ill-informed ideas about depression. I had been taught that depression was internalised anger and I believed that any medication for depression was just mood-altering stuff and probably a way of avoiding dealing with the real issues. There have been a significant number of people suffering depression in my pastoral care over the years. I can only pray that God will make it up to them for the ham-fisted way I've gone about advising and praying for them.

Before I realised I was in depression, I felt disappointed in myself over the way I had come to have little energy or enthusiasm for spiritual disciplines. My habit was to keep a daily journal, read some scripture and part of a devotional book and pray at certain times each day, but all this went by the board. Feelings of guilt rose up, but I couldn't be bothered to respond to them. I just felt flat. While thinking I could cut corners in my inner life and probably get away with it for a while, I tried harder than ever to kickstart myself into ministry activity. Everything was a real effort, even the things I normally enjoyed doing. All I really wanted to do was to escape from people and sleep. Preaching was especially difficult.

I remember, one Sunday morning, I went down to my office early to read over my sermon. I felt very down but I was sure that what I had to say was right and important. As I prayed it through, I started crying and couldn't stop. I had no idea what was happening, but guessed that I must just be really moved by my topic, 'Redeemed by the Son'.

Thinking that I had got the tears out of my system, I stood up to preach in the service, but the tears came again, stronger than ever. I tried hard to control myself but couldn't. In the end, I gave it up and someone else closed the service. Some people thought that 'the Spirit was moving on me' or that I had been convicted of something or was moved by compassion for the unredeemed in their plight. There were some very creative interpretations! The sad thing was that no one actually asked me what I thought was going on. I could not have told them, but it would have been nice if they had listened instead of assuming that they knew what was going on. That's another story.

I spent a couple of days reflecting on it and concluded that I was in trouble emotionally and had better back off. A few days later, I found myself in Archibald Hart's seminar about personal growth for ministers and his talk on depression. Great timing! I read his book, *Dark Clouds, Silver Linings* (Focus on the Family, 1993), and found it tremendously helpful.

After accepting that I was in depression, that the form of depression I was experiencing was a normal reaction to loss and that I was meant to be taking time for healing, I relaxed about my condition, deciding to let the depression take its course. Far from pestering me about not putting enough effort into prayer and Bible reading, God seemed to be very understanding. I felt loved by him, totally and unconditionally. He was watching over me, giving me time to grieve and adjust. This could be a risky way to relate to God in the long term, but it was just right for that period.

Words from Psalms 42 and 43 rang true for me:

Why are you downcast, O my soul?
Why so disturbed within me?
Put your hope in God, for I will yet praise him,
my Saviour and my God.

These words express well the conversation that was going on within me. I was indeed asking myself the question, 'Why are you downcast?' I needed to figure out what losses had contributed to my condition, so that I could bring them to God for comfort and healing, and I was reminding myself to rely on God and look forward to the day when I could once again praise him with heartfelt emotion. I was a long way from feeling any spiritual vitality at that point, but I clung to the hope that it would come back again in time.

Hart wrote that one sort of depression is a reaction to loss, and I could relate to this. Over the previous year and a half, two of my colleagues in ministry had left the church. One had caused tremendous difficulties for me before he left; the other was a very good friend and a great loss to the church and to me personally. Several other friends and supporters had left the church, almost all of them to take up ministries in other places. We had been empowering them for these moves, and I should have been delighted and fulfilled, but it just hurt to say goodbye.

With all these folk leaving, extra responsibility had fallen on me. As a consequence, I'd had to decline an invitation to serve a term as President of our denomination. Even though it would have taken considerable time, I would have enjoyed serving in this role, as well as the recognition and honour that came with it. It was my decision to pull out, but several influential members of the church had suggested I do so, putting considerable pressure on me. I still think it was the right move under the circumstances, but I was disappointed that others had not appreciated the sacrifice I was making. Perhaps it should not have been as big a deal for me as it was.

Another loss I was dealing with was less specific, yet it saddened me profoundly. I'd had a sense that God was saying, 'It's over.' What this meant to me was that the golden era of growth, creativity and community impact that my church had been experiencing for ten years had come to an end. I'd cried many tears over the thought that the church I had loved so much would never be the same again. All churches go through these cycles, and I knew that it was necessary for old things to pass away so that new things could come, but this knowledge did not comfort me.

Although it seems a bit silly, I also felt in all of this a loss of youth. As I was approaching 40 years of age, it could be said that I'd lost my youth some time before. Well, that may be true, but these were the thoughts that were in my head as I considered the losses that had contributed to my reactive depression.

The turning point came when I read Philippians 3:7–10 with this new concept of depression being linked to loss: 'I consider everything a loss compared to the surpassing greatness of knowing Christ Jesus my Lord' (v. 8). Those words helped me more than I can express. I'd read them many times and preached them too, but Hart's book gave me a new lens through which to see them. I talked about these things with some close friends and that was a great help. They acted as my counsellors, listening and asking good questions.

My time of depression became a time of rich learning. Not only did I come to understand more clearly what depression is, but I began to identify with my fellow sufferers. I learned not to be demanding of others or myself when depression comes, but to be gentle and patient. The lesson was reinforced for me that I should not assume I know what is going on for someone before I have thoroughly listened to him or her. I learned to watch out for warning signs in myself and to take seriously the concerns of those closest to me. Above all, I learned in a fresh and deep way about the beauty of God's grace, kindness and understanding.

10

Psalm 69:
The depths of unjust suffering

This is a rather long psalm and I have chosen not to include the text for that reason, but I would encourage you to have it open alongside you as you read this chapter. It is not familiar and I doubt if you have ever heard a sermon preached from it. You may never have heard it read aloud in church or listened to it set to music. It hardly fits the mould of the sort of passage that we like to use in worship—beautiful words, uplifting thoughts and comfort guaranteed. Don't be taken in by the heading either. It may be sung to the tune of 'Lilies', but this is no gentle lyric from *The Sound of Music*. No, this is a genuine lament. It is raw, honest, angry and disturbing. It comes from a deep place and reflects the genuine struggle of a sincere believer—and yet, despite its harshness, it is the second most quoted psalm in the New Testament.

The lament

Psalm 69 is ascribed to David, and this authorship is seemingly confirmed by the apostle Paul in Romans 11:9–10 (quoting 69:22–23). Although we know of nothing in David's life that fits the situation described here, this does not mean that the song could not have been penned by him. The issue behind the psalm is of unjust suffering, and this was certainly often David's personal experience. The writer is a person of sincere faith and spiritual zeal (v. 9) who finds himself wrongly accused of stealing (v. 4). Grogan aptly summaries the lament in verses 1–5: 'Here is a cry of desperation, vividly presented as coming from a man drowning in deep, fast-flowing water with a miry bottom, shrieking for help to one for whom he looks in vain until he is so hoarse he is hardly heard.'[18]

David is sure of his innocence but knows he is not perfect. He has made mistakes in his life, which he openly acknowledges: 'You know my folly, O God; my guilt is not hidden from you' (v. 5). He is concerned not just for his reputation and integrity, but for the impact of his situation on others, whom he does not wish to see stumble in their faith (v. 6). He is taken aback by the cruelty of his accusers, who seem to hate him without good reason and are determined to cause his downfall (v. 4). Even his family members have kept their distance in this time of turmoil (v. 8). The emotional cost is high and he is suffering inner pain and turmoil that threaten to overwhelm him. He feels scorned, shamed, disgraced— words that reflect a specific and profound anguish of heart. When he looks for sympathy and support, no one is there for him; he is alone and broken-hearted (v. 20).

As if this sad description of David's pain is not enough, there lies behind his words an implied criticism of God. It seems as if God is doing nothing to relieve his suffering but remains silent and inactive. 'My eyes fail, looking for my God (v. 3)' suggests that he has wept much but can cry no more as he waits for God to intervene. He has fasted and prayed and yet nothing seems to change (vv. 10–12). This spiritual agony only intensifies his suffering.

I wonder if you have ever been wrongly accused of something or suffered unjustly at the hands of other people. Have you been mistreated, abused or taken advantage of? Have people turned against you, criticised you unfairly or placed you outside the circle of friendship? Does it seem to you that there is no justice in the world? If so, you will have sympathy with David's predicament and understand his emotions. Some Christians are troubled by such an honest expression of pain and frustration, as if it denies the love of God or is merely an expression of self-pity, but to bring our pain to God in the context of prayer is a legitimate and healing response to suffering. Timothy Keller counsels us against making light of people's sorrow and grief by saying 'Pull yourself together'. He regrets the absence of freedom for lament in today's church and says, 'We should not assume that if we are trusting in God we won't weep or feel anger, or feel hopeless... The point is this—suffering people need to be able to weep and pour out their hearts, and not to immediately be shut down by being told what to do.'[19]

The causes of unjust suffering are not limited to false accusations. Sometimes life itself is unfair and we can feel that we have been given a raw deal by God. Things don't work out as we expect they should, and, compared to other people, we seem to have more than our fair share of suffering. A child is born disabled, a parent dies while still young, tragedy strikes randomly... you will have your own list. Lying behind this feeling of unfairness are those ancient questions, 'Why do bad things happen to good people?' and 'Why do good things happen to bad people?' Other psalms (such as Psalms 37 and 73) wrestle with these questions and many writers have attempted to answer the questions about suffering and a God of love. Here we simply underline the reality that suffering almost always seems unjust, and in the midst of it God can appear both silent and inactive.

For the person of faith, this is perhaps the hardest burden to bear. We pray for help and comfort but there is no response. All we need is a little word of encouragement and yet heaven remains silent, offline, uncommunicative. What is more, in the face of injustice, the God of justice seems to do nothing. Wrongdoers seem to be immune from divine censure, free to trample over the godly and continue their sinful ways unimpeded. Just a tap on the wrist would be enough, but God seems paralysed or apathetic. What is going on?

We are not to interpret the silence and inactivity of God as indicating a lack of awareness or interest in what is happening to us. On the contrary, he is deeply interested in us, but especially from the perspective of what is being formed within us through our times of suffering. He could intervene at once, but timing is everything with God and he will not speak or act until the time is right. It is true to say that he suffers with us in the waiting, for he does not want to cause us unnecessary pain, but he knows we have greater resources to endure than we realise, and so he will not preempt the process of refinement that is taking place in our hearts by bringing premature deliverance.

The picture of refining gold or silver is a common scriptural way of understanding suffering (Psalm 66:10; Proverbs 17:3; 27:21; Jeremiah 9:7; Zechariah 13:9; Malachi 3:2–3; 1 Peter 1:7). In the fire of the furnace, impurities in the metal are brought to the surface and then scraped away so that the metal becomes purer and more valuable. Unjust suffering is just one way by which God tests and refines our hearts, for the pain of it brings to the surface things that are hidden from view. Unhelpful attitudes and wrong beliefs are exposed. We see our selfishness and self-righteousness, our need to be in control and always right, our vindictiveness and impatience, our self-absorption and pride, and our demanding nature. But other qualities are being produced in us, too, like humility and compassion, understanding and forgiveness, endurance and perseverance, trust and dependence upon God. God knows what he is doing, even when he is apparently silent and inactive. Ultimately he is making us into better people, wiser people, and people more like his Son.

The surprise

The surprise is that Jesus is to be found right here in this deepest of laments. Apart from Psalm 22, no other psalm has as many links with the life of Christ or his suffering and death. Here are the cross references so that you can see the connections:

My throat is parched (v. 3)	John 19:28: 'I am thirsty'
Those who hate me without reason (v. 4)	John 15:25: a direct quote by Jesus
A stranger to my brothers (v. 8)	John 7:5: 'His own brothers did not believe in him'
Zeal for your house consumes me (v. 9)	John 2:17: direct quote, remembered by his disciples
The insults of those who insult you (v. 9)	Romans 15:3: direct quote by Paul about Jesus
Scorned, disgraced and shamed (v. 19)	Hebrews 12:2: the shame of the cross
Vinegar for my thirst (v. 21)	Matthew 27:34, 48: Wine vinegar given to Jesus on the cross

What this means, firstly, is that David was not alone in his suffering, even if it felt that way. We can say that Jesus was with him, an unseen presence sharing in his experience. We remember the story of Daniel's three friends in the fiery furnace, and how the onlookers saw four men in the flames, one 'like a son of the gods' accompanying the three Jews (Daniel 3:13–27). We may conclude that when we are in the midst of fiery trials, Jesus is there with us too, even if he is hidden from the naked eye or veiled to our understanding.

Secondly, David's experience, in some amazing way, prefigured the suffering of Christ. His suffering anticipated the way in which Jesus would be wrongly accused by his enemies, even predicting some of his actual physical sufferings. But more than that, Jesus in his sufferings identified himself with our sufferings, taking our sorrows upon himself (Isaiah 53:4). He has trodden where David trod, and he has lived our life and felt what we feel. This means he is fully able to sympathise with us and to be a merciful and faithful high priest on our behalf, interceding for us and pouring his grace into our lives on a daily basis (Hebrews 2:14–18; 4:14–16; 7:23–25). We can count on this divine aid, especially in the midst of suffering. He knows and he understands, and he is able to help and sustain us.

We may not always be able to give a reason for suffering, but, if we can find meaning within it, then we will be better able to cope with it and be changed by it. Part of the meaning is that through our experience of unjust suffering we are drawn closer to Christ, for we can appreciate his sufferings at the hands of sinful men and women; we begin to realise what he went through on our behalf, even if only in a small measure, and our love for him increases. Further, we can identify ourselves with him even more fully, experi-

encing what Paul calls 'the fellowship of sharing in his sufferings' (Philippians 3:10), an intimacy born out of a shared
pain. When we suffer unjustly or for the sake of Christ, we
become one with him in his ongoing suffering in the world
(Colossians 1:24). Michael Wilcock reassuringly reminds us,
'If that kind of disorientation is your nightmare, Christ has
been through it before you, and for you.'[20] Thus our walk
with God is deepened in the midst of even the darkest night.

The turnaround

David's experience as reflected in this psalm definitely fits the
life–death–resurrection pattern, and we see the movement
from lament to praise worked out in the struggle it describes.
Such a movement comes neither quickly nor easily, but it does
eventually come. It starts from somewhere deep within him
as prayer begins to rise to God again. Life may have contradicted the truth of God's covenant love, and his experience
denied it, but he has never let go of it (Psalm 145:8–9). 'But
I pray to you' suggests a change of momentum, a moment
of spiritual grace that enables him to transcend his circumstances and once again call on the name of the Lord. His cry
to God reveals the two anchors of his soul.

The first is the greatness of God's love. David can cry out
for rescue because of God's sure salvation. He is in the grip
of grace, and he knows now that, when the time comes, God
will act on his behalf, even if not in the way he imagined or
would prefer: 'But I pray to you, O Lord, in the time of your
favour; in your great love, O God, answer me with your sure
salvation' (69:13). The second is the goodness of God's love.
David knows that God will answer eventually because he is
a good God, one who is merciful and gracious and will not

turn his face away: 'Answer me, O Lord, out of the goodness of your love; in your great mercy turn to me' (v. 16). With these two anchors he is fastened to the Rock that cannot move and remains secure, despite the trial he is facing.

Letting off steam

As if to prove that the spiritual journey from lament to praise follows no straightforward path, David now presents us with a sudden outburst of anger and vitriol (vv. 22–28). Some would say that such a response is out of place on the lips of a person of faith. It is this part of the psalm that causes it to be classified among the 'imprecatory psalms', those that include an element of cursing and outspoken anger against either God or other people.[21] What are we to make of this? Is it appropriate for a Christian to pray in this way?

It seems to me that this outburst is like the lancing of a boil. Pressure has been building up inside David and is now released, and this needs to happen as part of the cleansing of his soul. It is perhaps best to look at it from the standpoint of his humanity. Emotions, even negative ones, are better expressed than repressed, and we can see this episode as a cathartic experience. In getting in touch with his feelings by writing them down, David begins to negate their influence. He is a man in great pain and distress (v. 29), and people under prolonged stress often speak and act thoughtlessly and without restraint. It is not surprising that someone who has been treated in the way that David has should feel the need for justice and payback. We may not always have spoken it out, but many of us will have had similar thoughts at some time in our lives against those who have mistreated or abused us. To censor such thoughts and deny their existence can be as harmful as expressing them inappropriately.

In defence of David, his outburst is not personal and he does not name individuals. He is not about to exact his own revenge. Instead he speaks to God and hands his case over to him (see also Romans 12:17–21). I have a feeling that once he had voiced his complaint, his anger subsided and the sting was taken out of his fury. Perhaps he gained a better perspective as a result and could calm down. Maybe, as he reflected on his outburst, he saw exposed his own self-righteousness and superiority, his need for revenge. Could it be that he caught a glimpse of the violence within, his desire to hurt those who had hurt him? Did he afterwards regret his words?

In cultures like my own, where anger is not usually expressed openly, to pray in this way seems strange and offensive, even sub-Christian. The culture in which the psalm was written, however, like many other cultures worldwide, is not given to such polite reserve; it is expressive, passionate and emotional, given to exaggeration. Perhaps we read too much into these verses when we read them through our own cultural glasses. Isn't it right that we should be passionate about justice and let God know that we are unhappy with injustice? Perhaps those of us who do not get worked up are the ones who are at fault. One thing is for sure: God has allowed these outbursts to be recorded, so we can learn from them. This does not mean he gives approval to everything expressed here, but it does suggest that he does not mind when we are fired up in his presence. He prefers his people to be either hot or cold, rather than lukewarm (Revelation 3:16). We have divine permission to be open in conversation with God, and thus find the grace to surrender our need for justice and our feelings of hatred and aggression to the one who is ultimately the Judge of us all.

Thanksgiving

We cannot say what kind of time interval there was between verses 29 and 30, but the change from pain and distress to song and thanksgiving did not come about immediately. Prayer has been answered and the boil has been lanced, and perhaps, too, counsel has been given. Several biblical scholars hold to the idea that the mood changes we see here and in several other psalms (as noted earlier, for example, in Psalm 130) reflect the giving of counsel from a priest or prophet. This is conjecture, but it reminds us that the timely help of a wise friend or spiritual director can be a great asset to anyone finding their way through a spiritual crisis. Whatever has taken place, David is now on the resurrection side of the valley; the waters have subsided and the sun is shining again. Either his situation has been resolved or, by God's grace, he has come to peace about it.

David declares, 'I will praise God's name in song and glorify him with thanksgiving' (v. 30). Thanksgiving is a most powerful spiritual dynamic, and it is important, if we have seen our prayers answered or have received grace in our time of need, that we make sure we express our gratitude in praise to God. Jesus emphasised this discipline (Luke 17:11–19), and so did the apostle Paul (Colossians 3:15–17, 1 Thessalonians 5:18), and, of course, the Psalms are full of such examples (103:1–5; 118:18–21). We know that our feet are standing on solid ground again when a song of praise comes readily to our lips.

A renewed sense of gratitude is one of the outcomes of a period of spiritual transition, as is a new revelation of spiritual truth—for example, the radical realisation that heart praise is more acceptable to God than external religious ritual and sacrifice (v. 31). There often also comes a new assurance about old truths, authenticated now by personal experience and gladly shared with others: 'The poor will see and be glad—you who seek God, may your hearts live! The Lord hears the needy and does not despise his captive people' (vv. 32–33). This, of course, brings David back in line with the foundational truth of Psalm 145:18: 'The Lord is near to all who call on him, to all who call on him in truth.' He is at home again.

As in many of the psalms of lament, the ending takes us to the community of faith, the nation of Israel and the wider world. It may be that verses 34–36 are a later addition, for they seem to refer to the period of the exile, when David was no longer around. What they tell us is that there is hope for Israel as well. One day the people will return from exile and rebuild their cities. They will resettle the land, along with their children, and will once again live out their lives as those who love God. They may be in the period of 'death' at the moment, but, just as the faithful God gave 'resurrection' to David in times past, so he will one day give 'resurrection' to his people. This reminder to them can serve as a reminder to us as well.

* * *

One of the hardest experiences in life, for any parent, is to see their child suffer. That really does seem unjust and unfair, and coming to terms with it is very difficult. Daniel and Damaris, a young couple living and working in Africa, faced such a challenge to their faith, and have had to walk a path that no one would choose.

11

Samara's story

It was already late in the pregnancy when we noticed that our baby was not normal. There was a growth retardation that caused the doctors concern and, in the end, required an early delivery at 35 weeks. Blood tests confirmed that our tiny 1.2 kg baby had rubella. This disease has been almost eradicated in the Western world but in Eastern Africa it is still very common. Despite the required vaccinations, my wife Damaris had contracted the disease: the chances were as big as those of winning the lottery.

After Samara had spent seven weeks in an incubator, we were allowed to take her home. By this point, we knew that she had three heart defects and was developing cataracts in her eyes, both problems common to babies born with rubella. We did our best to settle into a routine, but, after some communication with eye specialists in Germany, we found out that we needed to rush to Germany to save our daughter's eyesight. Within two days we had packed our things and obtained a passport for Samara and were on a flight to Germany, fearful of what awaited us.

We expected a six-week stay for Samara's eye surgery and a general check-up. This was not to be, however, and over the next 15 months we were in and out of the hospital. One of the first shocks was the discovery that Samara was also severely hearing-impaired and had apparently heard nothing of the songs we had sung to her. We also found out that her heart was much worse than we had previously thought. Doctors told us they could do a non-invasive procedure to fix her heart and assured us the operation was 95 per cent successful. Well, we fell in the other five per cent: it didn't work. Samara needed open-heart surgery at six months, weighing 3 kg. The disappointments continued as she developed liver and lung problems and stopped eating, relying fully on the feeding tube. Every time we thought we could prepare to go back to the mission field, new issues would arise. Samara had to suffer a total of nine surgeries in 15 months. It was a difficult time for our small family, to say the least.

Thoughts of a father

As a father, I had expectations of how I would be able to love, care for, protect and nurture our first child, Samara. I remember the day when we found out that our little girl had heart issues. It was early days and only the tip of the iceberg, but for me it brought the realisation that our lives were not going to be the way we had expected. I realised that our child would probably never be healthy, and that we would have to deal with this for the rest of our lives. That day was the only day I cried.

Some months later, in Germany, I was waiting for the open-heart surgery that was to take place the following day. I was not allowed to stay with my wife and daughter in the hospital and sat alone, looking out of the window, wondering if God cared at all. I wondered if Samara would die from the surgery and if my wife would be able to handle the situation, which was becoming unbearable. Once again I could do nothing, and that sense of helplessness made me angry. To see your child suffer is something that should never happen.

I would have happily taken her place, but could not.

We spent many days waiting—waiting for results, waiting for doctors, waiting for surgery to be done, always waiting. It is not in my nature to wait, and the waiting didn't get easier; we just got used to the process. Often I asked myself what sort of timeframe God was on, and the verse that says, 'One day is like a thousand years and a thousand years are like a day' was no help at all. Did God have any idea what it was like to live 'now', in the moment, with fear, uncertainty and worry?

We don't have the benefit of a big picture, as he does— but, then again, Jesus lived with the same limitations that we have. He dealt with the fear of 'now' in the garden of Gethsemane, when he struggled with the task ahead of him. The process of living is a lot harder than talking or writing about it. 'Save me, O God, for the waters have come up to my neck' (Psalm 69:1). I read that verse now with an understanding born of suffering and, to be honest, I sometimes wish I did not have so much in common with the psalmist.

Thoughts of a mother

From the moment I knew that Samara had rubella, I chose to believe that God would protect her from all that the diagnosis entailed. In the few minutes I was allowed to hold her outside the incubator, I prayed over the different parts of her body, blessed her and trusted that God would heal her completely. I had faith! But, as the situation with Samara kept going from bad to worse, I started wondering whether prayer was of any use. We had an army of over 300 people praying with us for Samara and nothing seemed to be getting better. 'I am worn out calling for help; my throat is parched. My eyes fail, looking for my God' (Psalm 69:3). Every day we prayed the same prayers but we couldn't see God intervening. At some point we stopped praying for healing and just asked for strength to cope with whatever happened.

I'd always heard that hard times bring you closer to God, but this hardship made me feel further away from him than ever. Through it all, I lost my sense of trust in Jesus. The promise that God 'never gives us more than we can bear' felt untrue. Yes, I knew God was in control but I wanted to feel his comfort and peace in my soul, which would make me feel better. 'Do not let… the depths swallow me up... Answer me, O Lord' (vv. 15–16). But the comfort didn't come. I stood at my girl's hospital bed, praying for her to have a restful night. Then, as I said 'Amen', she had one of her stomach attacks and threw up so badly that I spent the next half-hour cleaning up both her and the bed and another few hours walking up and down the corridor to calm her down again. Are you even listening to me, God? Why won't you help?'

I still have questions and I still don't understand how God works at times. I don't know why he didn't take some of the suffering away from my tiny little girl and why he didn't give me the comfort I longed for so desperately. But I do know he was there. I know he made our girl strong to fight through it all, he brought wonderful people into our lives to help us and he gave us promises to cling to.

The name 'Samara' just came to me one day and, after realising that it means 'protected by God', we knew that this was his promise over her life. When she was born, I was reading through Mark 4 and 5 and knew God was telling me that my 'little mustard seed', the tiniest of all, was going to grow into a big tree. He was going to say to her, 'Little girl, I say to you, get up!' as he did to the daughter of Jairus, and she would.

Even now, when we can't see God's intervening hand in the struggles we still face, I cling on to the encouragement that our friends in Kenya gave us before we left: when you can't see God's hand, trust his heart. 'In your great love, O God, answer me with your sure salvation' (Psalm 69:13). God's heart is to love and to save and I want to trust him, even through suffering.

12

Psalm 88:
The depths of darkness

Of all the songs of lament in the book of Psalms, this has to be the saddest. It is a psalm that takes us into the deepest darkness, where all sense of the presence of God has been lost and the writer feels alone, abandoned and forgotten. It is not a place I have ever been to myself, nor do I want to go there; I guess you don't, either. Yet some are called to go through such an experience, and, in the loving wisdom of God, it is a place of significant spiritual formation where we may discover the treasures of darkness (Isaiah 45:3).

The psalm is attributed to Heman the Ezrahite, and he appears to have been in the musical guild known as the Sons of Korah. He may be talking about his own experience or that of someone else. The painful circumstances that the psalm reflects could easily describe the experience of Uzziah (2 Chronicles 26:21), Hezekiah (Isaiah 38:9–20), Jeremiah or Job. Perhaps that is the point. This *maskil* (a teaching song) is meant to have a widespread application. Brueggemann, who considers it to be 'an embarrassment to conventional faith', summarises it like this:

It is the cry of a believer (who sounds like Job) whose life has gone awry, who desperately seeks contact with God but who is unable to evoke a response from God. This is indeed 'the dark night of the soul' when the troubled person must be, and must stay, in the darkness of abandonment, utterly alone.[22]

The 'dark night of the soul' is a prolonged experience in which God appears to be absent; it can last weeks, months or even years. Many of us will have times when the presence of God is not very real to us, but this represents a full-blown breakdown of all the normal ways we encounter him: worship becomes flat, Bible reading is dull, fellowship seems boring and the heart is cold. It was first described by St John of the Cross (1542–91) as part of the spiritual journey, a stage through which a person may pass on the way to union with God. It is a painful experience of 'depression and desolation, of feeling abandoned by God and yet longing for God', given to those whom God wants to draw even closer to himself.[23] Should you find yourself in such a place of darkness, take it as a compliment from God: he is entrusting you with something special, he knows you have the inner resources to cope with it, and he is bringing you into a deeper intimacy with himself.

Most people around the world will be aware of Mother Teresa and her work among the poor in Calcutta. Her life touched many people and she is one Christian who would be known and admired by almost everyone. What many do not realise, however, is that much of her life was lived in 'the dark night of the soul'. We know from her diaries that although she went about her duties cheerfully and happily, she was often devoid of any inner sense of God's nearness.

She wrote in a note to her spiritual director:

Now Father—since 49 or 50 this terrible sense of loss—this untold darkness—this loneliness—this continual longing for God—

which gives me that pain deep down in my heart. Darkness is such that I really do not see—neither with my mind nor with my reason. The place of God in my soul is blank—There is no God in me. When the pain of longing is so great—I just long & long for God—and then it is that I feel—He does not want me—He is not there... God does not want me—Sometimes— I just hear my own heart cry out—'My God' and nothing else comes—The torture I can't explain.[24]

Perhaps God was able to use Mother Teresa so wonderfully because she had sought him so earnestly and found him in the deep places of her own soul. We may envy people whom God uses greatly, without realising that often they have paid a great price. Death has been at work in them, so that life may be at work in others (2 Corinthians 4:7–12).

When we look at the structure of Psalm 88, we can see immediately a simple pattern that looks like this:

- Verses 1–2: Prayer to the God who saves me
- Verse 3–8: Forsaken by God
- Verse 9: Calling to God every day
- Verses 10–12: Bewildered by God
- Verse 13: A cry for help in the morning
- Verses 14–18: Rejected by God

This very structure has something to teach us. We must never simply surrender to the darkness or become passive. No matter how bad we feel, we must continue to do the things that are right, to maintain our spiritual discipline, just as Mother Teresa did.

Faith in the midst of total darkness

While the psalm describes a sense of spiritual loss greater than most of us will ever know, and a darkness that seems unending (vv. 6, 12, 18), even when there is nothing to encourage him the writer never lets go of the basic spiritual discipline of prayer. His conviction that God is the one who saves him has not wavered, and, although there is no response from God, he continues with his rhythm of prayer: 'O Lord, the God who saves me, day and night I cry out before you. May my prayer come before you; turn your ear to my cry' (vv. 1–2). For this man of faith, prayer is the offering of himself to God, and this he does daily: 'I call to you, O Lord, every day; I spread out my hands to you' (v. 9). Each new day brings the hope of breakthrough, the promise of relief and release: 'But I cry to you for help, O Lord; in the morning my prayer comes before you' (v. 13).

What this psalm does not promise is that there we will always receive an immediate response to our prayers. Believers can remain in darkness for a long time, not because of sin or lack of faith on their part, but simply because God is doing something within them during the period of apparent absence. At such times it is helpful to maintain our spiritual disciplines, regardless of how we feel and the seeming inconsistency between our actions and our feelings. This is not hypocrisy but walking by faith. One of the desert fathers, Isaac of Nineveh (who died about AD700), apparently told his monastic followers not to be perturbed if they encountered times of darkness, but to wait it out. He advised them, 'Wrap your head in your cloak and sleep, until the hour of darkness is over, but do not leave your cell.'[25] Sometimes waiting is all we can do.

Forsaken by God (vv. 3–9a)

For my soul is full of trouble
and my life draws near the grave.
I am counted among those who go down to the pit;
I am like a man without strength.
I am set apart with the dead,
like the slain who lie in the grave,
whom you remember no more,
who are cut off from your care.
You have put me in the lowest pit,
in the darkest depths.
Your wrath lies heavily upon me;
you have overwhelmed me with all your waves.
You have taken from me my closest friends
and have made me repulsive to them.
I am confined and cannot escape;
my eyes are dim with grief.

Here the writer communicates his anguish through the use of vivid metaphors associated with death and dying. His life is full of trouble, and the worst thing is that God appears to be uncaring and indifferent to his plight. It is God whom he holds responsible for this state of affairs. God has brought him into 'the darkest depths'—perhaps, he surmises, because he is angry with him. The psalmist feels overwhelmed, drowning in a sea of grief. Maybe he is suffering physical illness, like Job with his boils or Uzziah with his leprosy. Certainly his friends don't want to know him. He feels alone and abandoned, with no way of escape. God has cornered him and taken him captive.

Perhaps one aspect of God's strategy in this poor man's life is to wean him away from the 'attachments' of the world. We do not always recognise the hold that people and things have upon us until they are taken from us. This stripping away of the non-essentials in our lives can be compared to a tree in winter being denuded of its leaves. Only then is the beauty of its form really seen—the structure of the branches, the shape of the trunk. With the sun behind it and a blue sky overhead, a tree in winter is a glorious sight, but it can only be seen like this because it has lost its leaves. In its nakedness it possesses a glory otherwise unnoticed. Like-wise, the soul's beauty may not always be glimpsed in days of prosperity and ease; it takes adversity to reveal its true worth.

Bewildered by God (vv. 10–12)

Do you show your wonders to the dead?
Do those who are dead rise up and praise you?
Is your love declared in the grave,
your faithfulness in Destruction?
Are your wonders known in the place of darkness,
or your righteous deeds in the land of oblivion?

One of the characteristics of those of us brought up in the world of modernity is that we expect to understand everything. We must be able to explain things, to fathom them out, to find a reason for what happens. In short, we must be able to make sense of life. When we can't do that, we are confused and we flounder. God, however, cannot be subjected to human reason. Our tiny brains could never comprehend him or fathom his plans (Isaiah 55:8–9; Romans 11:33–36; 1 Corinthians 1:18–20). The dark night enables us to come to terms with this reality, to allow God to remain beyond our understanding, and to be content to trust him on the basis of his character rather than our reasoning. When we come to this point, we have reached a significant milestone in our spiritual growth. It is all right not to know, to be comfortable with a degree of mystery.

In these verses, the psalmist is responding to his plight rather like a lawyer in a court of law, cross-examining his witness. To all logical understanding, God is making a mistake. Surely it would be better if the psalmist were free to praise God as before, to declare his love to others, to make known the wonders of God and his righteous deeds to the world? The argument is persuasive to human reason, and the picture it paints of the 'normal' life of faith is appealing, yet his plea seems to hold no sway in heaven, for God is interested in something more. At this moment, God is more concerned with who the psalmist is becoming and the changes taking place in his soul that will make him even more effective in his service later on. For now, the agenda is transformation, and darkness is the context for change (see Romans 8:28–29). God will not be deflected from his stated purpose.

Rejected by God (vv. 14–18)

Why, O Lord, do you reject me
and hide your face from me?
From my youth I have been afflicted and close to death;
I have suffered your terrors and am in despair.
Your wrath has swept over me;
your terrors have destroyed me.
All day long they surround me like a flood;

they have completely engulfed me.
You have taken my companions and loved ones from me;
the darkness is my closest friend.

Once more we feel the psalmist's anguish, in particular his loneliness and isolation. This feeling of being rejected and unworthy of love seems to have troubled him throughout his life, and now his sense of rejection is transferred to God. He imagines a God who is punitive and unfeeling, more likely to chastise than to heal. He is not yet at home with the idea of the covenant-keeping God of mercy and grace (Psalm 145:8–9), but this is the truth he needs to discover, and only when he has faced up to his own inner pain can he find the healing he so desperately needs.

Psychologist David Benner has written helpfully about the need for us all to live in the reality of who we are, not with some 'ideal' self or 'make-believe' me. All of us are good at hiding from reality and pretending to be who we are not, but God is a God of truth and wants us to become our true selves, the persons he made us to be. Benner writes:

> *The path of life will invariably take us through experiences we would never choose—experiences of depression, failure, illness, suffering, betrayal, abuse, neglect, anger, doubt, confusion, and eventually death. If we seek to avoid the experience of these dark places, we will lose contact with important dimensions of our being... But when we dare to face those demons in the dark places of our interior self, we discover that life can be lived with more intensity, passion, and clarity of vision.*[26]

It seems to me that this is what happens in the experience of the 'dark night'. God presents us with an opportunity to leave our unreality behind and courageously step into a new life of authenticity and truth. Benner continues, 'The things I view as crises in my life will usually be the very things that I need in order to draw me out of my fearful hiding from reality. These things have the power to break apart the illusions I have spun around my being and remake me from the foundations.'[27]

'The darkness is my closest friend' (v. 18). Here is the closing thought in this challenging psalm. At first sight it seems to end on a sad note—unusual even for the psalms of lament, which normally see at least some progression towards a resolution of the crisis and a note of optimism. It suggests that issues are not always easily resolved, which is an important insight. However, there may be something more positive in mind here. Mother Teresa was able to say, 'For the first time in this eleven years—I have come to love this darkness—for I believe now that it is a part, a very, very small part of Jesus' darkness and pain on earth.'[28] Maybe the psalmist too is beginning to realise that the darkness is actually working to his advantage.

What, then, are the positives that we can see in the 'dark night of the soul'? Firstly, they have to include this insight, this sharing in the sufferings of Christ of which Mother Teresa spoke. On the cross, Jesus cried out with the words of Psalm 22:1: 'My God, my God, why have you forsaken me?' Matthew (27:46) records these words in Aramaic and notes that they were spoken at the ninth hour (3.00 pm) as darkness covered the land. In a way in which we can never fully understand, Jesus experienced abandonment by the Father as the sins of the whole world were laid upon him. We know that it was impossible for the Father to abandon the Son in an absolute sense (Acts 2:27; Psalm 16:10), but it appears that, in this moment when sin was being dealt with, it was necessary for a holy God to turn his face away. Thus Jesus experienced for our sakes the separation from God that we deserved, and, in doing so, made it possible for us to be brought back into relationship with God. He experienced the total darkness associated with the sin of the world. When we encounter darkness, we can use it to help us catch a glimpse, albeit a small one, of what he went through on the cross.

Writer and broadcaster Jane Grayshon speaks from a life lived with chronic pain and times of deep spiritual darkness, as she has faced severe illness and been close to death. She has discovered that God can be found in the darkness, and, indeed, has come to believe that just as seeds are hidden in darkness underground in order to germinate, so there is a darkness that is essential for our spiritual growth. Even when we can see nothing of him, God does his most creative and important work in our darkness, too. Jane says that every little suffering carries the invitation for us to glimpse what Jesus went through, and thereby to share with him in his depths. Our pain, whatever kind of pain it is, can be an opportunity for us to feel with him. She writes, 'This is one of the treasures of darkness: that in our depths, in our darkness, we stumble upon the awe-filling truth. We are invited to share with Christ in his agony.'[29]

A second positive to emerge is that we begin to value God for God's own sake. It is a very subtle temptation, of which we are all guilty, to seek God for his blessings. This was the question that Satan asked God concerning Job: is it possible for a human being to love God for God's own sake? Satan's assumption was that if God removed his blessing from Job, Job would curse him to his face. God allowed Job to be put through the most severe trials because he knew that Job's faith was genuine. Eventually, after much agony, Job proved that his love for God was not dependent on being blessed by him. In some small way, all of us will be asked the same question, and life may well throw up a challenge to the purity of our own faith.

In a similar vein, and even more subtly, those of us who are people of faith can substitute other things for God. The experience of knowing God can mean more to us than knowing God himself. We can be addicted to the joy of the worship experience rather than being in love with God, or enamoured with studying the Bible or our gift of preaching instead of being hungry for him. This is why God sometimes has to expose our attachments, those things that take his place in our lives. When we are stripped of such externals, we are able to love God for God's own sake, to find our rest in God alone (Psalm 62:1, 5). Our dependence on other things for contentment is lessened and we discover a new joy in God himself.

Finally, the presence of this psalm within the scriptures is of great pastoral benefit. The writer may have wondered if his life had any meaning at all, and if any good could come from his suffering, yet even now his words bring comfort and relief to other burdened souls. Kidner comments, 'Burdened and despondent as he was, his existence was far from pointless. If it was a living death, in God's hands it was to bear much fruit.'[30] The psalmist's story shows that, for some, extended suffering may well mark out the path they are called to walk, but this does not mean that God is displeased with them or that they are lacking in faith. Because of his words, others find that their pain and abandonment, even their doubt, are validated as part of genuine Christian experience. God remains their God, not because they say and do all the right things but because he is their God and is gracious towards them.

* * *

James and Debbie have known times of darkness and extended suffering in their own lives. For them, there have been no easy answers or miraculous deliverance, but they have continued (with God's grace), to follow.

13

James and Debbie's story

We have both suffered with ME, otherwise known as Chronic Fatigue Syndrome, for over 20 years, and Debbie also had breast cancer diagnosed in 2010, for which she is now in remission.

ME has cast a dark shadow over our lives. It is a dreadful condition, the only predictable thing about it being its unpredictability. Both our careers were stopped abruptly in our mid-20s and for many years it seemed as if our lives were on permanent hold, while we gazed at our friends who had prospering careers, took on mortgages, got married and had families. It is very hard to believe that over half our lives have been affected by poor health. We are very glad that we did not know what lay ahead; we could never have imagined how difficult things would be for us.

ME is still a controversial disorder and the way it is viewed is in total contrast with the sort of condition that people can easily see, such as a broken leg or cancer. When Debbie was diagnosed with breast cancer, it became very apparent that cancer was viewed differently from ME within the medical profession. Although ME is not a life-threatening condition, it has lasted a lot longer than the cancer.

Early on in our ME, we both racked our brains to think of any unconfessed sin in our lives; at different times, other Christians have prayed against any occult involvement in previous generations of our families. We wondered if we ourselves might be responsible for our poor health because of a lack of faith. When we were very ill, we felt extremely vulnerable. We have learned through experience that there is no simple formula for success in praying for healing, or easy answers to the question of why we and many others suffer. Simplistic formulas for living the Christian life (such as 'obedience leads to blessings; disobedience leads to lack of blessings') do not work, and pat answers are unhelpful and hurtful to those who are suffering.

Of course, we wondered where God was in all this darkness and difficulty. Despite many prayers for healing, our outward lives have remained limited because of our ongoing health problems. We both believe that God heals people today and this belief can make chronic illness more difficult to understand, both for us and our family and friends. It is puzzling why, despite prayer ministry and days of fasting and prayer, our health does not seem to improve as much as we would like. We have been through many ups and downs—times when hopes are raised, then dashed again, bringing great disappointment. There have been welcome improvements, followed by relapses.

Suffering has a way of stripping away everything that is ultimately unimportant and focusing our attention completely on God. When our health, career and many of the things that are important to us are taken away, can we say, 'Lord, I don't know why you are allowing any of this, but I am going to trust you', even though it seems to make no sense? Despite the difficult times, we echo Peter's words, 'Lord, to whom shall we go? You have the words of eternal life' (John 6:68).

Having ME has involved dealing with a lot of loss in our lives—loss of health, income, careers, hobbies, social life and church involvement, as well as the chance to have children. We have found that this loss has involved a lot of grieving, which has been an ongoing process involving sadness, anger and emotional turmoil. We have learned that these feelings are completely normal, a natural reaction to loss. If only someone had told us this earlier! We have found that expressing and working through these feelings is the healthy, ultimately helpful way to deal with them, rather than burying them or pretending that they are not there because they seem 'unspiritual'.

Many of the psalms express questioning, suffering, disappointment, darkness and mystery, and it is reassuring to read the psalmists' honest expression of these feelings to God. It is true to say that all these emotions have been part of our experience over the last 20 years or so, and we suspect that many other Christians are wrestling with them as well. Some of the questions we have asked over the years are: What is God doing? Is it my sin that is to blame? Where is God in all this? Why is he allowing this? How long, O Lord? Does God want to heal me? Why does he not heal me? Are the things that I have been taught about God, life, faith and the Bible really true? Can I continue to believe God's promises in scripture in the way I have understood them in the past? Despite never losing our belief in God, at one stage our frequent thought was, 'I don't know what I believe any more.' God is big enough for us to ask him these questions. We need to be real. He is not upset when we are upset with him.

We have been very fortunate to be able to share our deepest feelings with each other. In the midst of suffering, having each other to journey with through our doubts, pain and loss has been more helpful than a comprehensive theological explanation for suffering. In some ways, that explanation emerged later, as we tried to make sense of things. Over the years we have developed a growing appreciation that when we go through these dark, difficult times, God is taking us deeper with him. He gives us 'treasures of darkness', priceless discoveries that we could not have found or come to know in the easy times. One of our most precious discoveries has been that who we are is more important that what we do, achieve or own. Our most important and truest identity is that we are, each one of us, God's beloved child.

We know from experience that minimising someone's suffering by saying that things are 'not as bad as they seem' can be very hurtful: often these times really are as dark, black and awful as they seem. One of the most difficult experiences was that God often appeared to be absent from us when we needed him the most. We have both endured long periods (for Debbie, at one stage, seven and a half years) when the felt sense of God's presence was removed. The sense of abandonment was intense and very painful. Prayer, Bible reading and worship felt empty, painful and unrewarding. We had read several books on adversity, but they did not seem to help.

Debbie says of her most prolonged period of the loss of God's presence:

At the time, I did not cope well with this. At the beginning I spent time just seeking to be with God and open myself up to him, crying out for help and for his touch. But these times were so painful, spiritually and emotionally, for me—because all I felt was emptiness and abandonment. I felt I couldn't continue with these times, so I rather shut my heart up to God. Although I carried on with joint devotional times with James and attended church when physically able, it just felt like going through the motions. God rarely seemed to speak to me and I did not feel anything of his presence. His promises seemed empty and prayer was painful. I felt as if something had died within me.

However, there did come a time for us when the felt sense of God's presence began to return, and there were several factors that were helpful. They included listening to reflective music, taking part in retreats and Quiet Days, learning more about contemplative prayer, scripture meditation, silence and stillness, and Celtic Christian spirituality. When we spend time with God in silence, it is OK if nothing appears to be happening. God is working and, over time, you realise you are changing and feeling differently about life.

We found it very helpful to learn more about spiritual formation and the development of the inner life, including some of the stages that God takes us through as we grow. We learned that there is often a process of deconstructing and then reconstructing what we believe about God, faith and our relationship with him. This process was very painful at the time but ultimately provided a way to grow, as it allowed us to know God better in the end. It has led to a stronger, more solid foundation for our relationship with God.

So where are we now?

We are learning that God is always good and we are always loved. Our outward circumstances are still not ideal: we are still living with ME and coming to terms with childlessness, and life often feels full of challenges. Over a period of time, though, we have been brought to a different place inwardly.

God has used the darkest times to shape us and make us more like his Son. We have found that allowing God to deal with us is the key to fruitfulness. Sometimes it is a bit like a corkscrew or a screw going into wood: we don't seem to be 'going' anywhere, but in fact we are drilling deeper all the time. No one would choose a path of suffering, but it enables us to reach out to others who are hurting, confused and on the edge of churches. We offer our weakness and vulnerability.

Change is a slow and painful process because we don't change easily. God is concerned about who we are becoming and he is never in a hurry. He can use even the worst of our circumstances to change and shape us. God suffers with us, collecting all our tears in his bottle (Psalm 56:8, NLT), but he also wants the very best for us, so sometimes he allows us to go through situations, knowing in advance that we might give up altogether. He loves us enough to risk losing our love, because he wants us to know him and his love ever more deeply.

In our moments of fear, uncertainty and weak faith, God has got hold of us and will not let us go. It is all grace, not of us. God says, 'Stay in my love. Don't worry about the rest; I'll take care of all the rest.' His grip on us is strong and secure: it is not a case of our strong grip on him. Even when we cannot keep ourselves, he keeps us. Even when we are faithless, he is faithful. Even the valley of tears can become a place of springs (Psalm 84:6).

14

Psalm 30:
A thanksgiving song

Reaching Psalm 30 after the darkness and despair of Psalm 88 is like waking up one morning to find that winter is over and spring has come. Grey clouds and a strong biting wind have given way to blue skies, bright sunshine and the singing of birds. It feels good to be alive again; hope has returned and once again we can smile and laugh.

Psalm 30 is one of the best examples of a psalm written after a time of disorientation. Here the writer has come out on the other side and is in a new period of reorientation. Lament gives way to thanksgiving. Trouble has come and gone; the enemies have been defeated. It is a time of victory. There is new buoyancy to his faith, a new confidence in his step and new insight into life with God. The psalmist writes with the wisdom that comes from lived experience.

The psalm is attributed to David, and there is no reason to doubt this authorship, although the precise circumstances behind the writing of the psalm remain, as often, somewhat vague. The ascription 'for the dedication of the temple' is puzzling, though, since it was Solomon, not David, who presided over its building. Some scholars suggest that for 'temple' we should read 'house', and refer us to 2 Samuel 5:11–12 and the building of David's royal palace. Others would see the context as being the arrival of the ark of the covenant in Jerusalem (2 Samuel 6:16–17). Whatever the specific occasion that prompted the writing of this psalm, the point is that it is a thanksgiving song describing a great deliverance, and is suitable for use by God's people on any future celebration of his goodness.

Testimony (vv. 1–3)

I will exalt you, O Lord,
for you lifted me out of the depths
and did not let my enemies gloat over me.
O Lord my God, I called to you for help
and you healed me.
O Lord, you brought me up from the grave;
you spared me from going down into the pit.

David begins rightly by giving praise to God. He is back on level ground, where praise is the norm and is once more part of his way of life (Psalm 145:1–2). This kind of praise has a deeper note to it, however, because it is occasioned by a remarkable deliverance brought about solely by divine intervention. The transformation in his fortunes has nothing to do with David; it has all to do with God. He has been surprised by grace, taken aback by the power of God operative on behalf of his undeserving self. Three striking metaphors are used to try to convey the significance of this deliverance.

- It has been a dramatic rescue ('you lifted me', v. 1). It was as if David had been thrown like a bucket into a well, with no means of escape until God reached down and lifted him to safety. The sense of having been 'lifted' out of danger is a common one in the Psalms (9:13; 40:2; 107:41).

- It has been an amazing healing ('you healed me', v. 2). Perhaps this verse refers to an actual experience of sickness, as do so many of the psalms of lament (for example, Psalm 6; 22; 31; 38; 41; 88), from which David has been miraculously healed. Alternatively, it may refer to a general sense of being healed spiritually (from sin), emotionally (from guilt and shame) and psychologically (from distorted thinking).
- It has been a powerful resurrection ('you brought me up', v. 3). It felt to David as if he were on the point of death when God stepped in and changed his fortunes. This remarkable turnaround confounded his enemies and took David by surprise. Whether it was a physical or emotional experience, it has filled him with awe and wonder at the power of God.

No wonder David turns his gratitude into thanksgiving, and his indebtedness to praise. Here is a statement of victory, not achieved but given—a celebration of a winning outcome that could so easily have ended in defeat. It aptly describes, too, the 'life–death–resurrection' pattern that we have been considering.

A lesson learned and an insight gained (vv. 4–5)

Sing praise to the Lord, you saints of his;
praise his holy name.
For his anger lasts only a moment,
but his favour lasts a lifetime;
weeping may remain for a night,
but rejoicing comes in the morning.

Not content to sing his own praise to God, David calls on other godly people to join him. 'Saints' is a translation of *hasidim*, a word linked to the Hebrew *hesed*, meaning 'covenant love'. The 'saints' are the faithful in Israel, those who are in a covenant relationship with God and know themselves loved by him. Such people would, of course, be delighted to join David in giving thanks to God, for his joy is their joy, and, as their king, it is right that he should lead them in praise of their covenant God. Together they can 'praise his holy name'—that is, delight in God's character and faithfulness.

David's experience of disorientation is not without its rewards. He has gained a new understanding of the character of God and a new insight into his ways. Now he proclaims to his fellow worshippers a truth of which he is living proof: God's discipline of his servants is only ever temporary, whereas his love and faithfulness are continuous. This truth can encourage all God's people who find themselves in the valley, and it is summed up beautifully in verse 5. This is a good example of parallelism, where the second line repeats and further explains the first; and the words used bounce off each other in contrasting thought (anger/favour with weeping/rejoicing; moment/lifetime with night/morning).

The first half of verse 5 looks at the experience of disorientation from God's perspective, and the temporary expression of his anger is contrasted with the permanent expression of his grace. I find that, in my retreats and teaching seminars, I have to explain God's anger very carefully to people, because many find it a difficult concept to deal with. Often people read into the word 'anger' (or, even more so, the word 'wrath') a human connotation of anger—an emotion that is harsh, uncontrolled, unpredictable, violent and so on. They project their own negative experience of angry people on to God and end up with a picture of a God who is capricious, bullying and likely to fly off the handle in a rage at our slightest misdemeanour. This is not a nice thought, and of course it is completely wrong and misleading. God's anger can in no way be compared to the human emotion of anger. It is, in fact, an expression of his love; it describes his passionate desire that we should experience the very best he has for us, and his determination that nothing should prevent our growth in grace. It can best be defined as his settled opposition to anything that is unhelpful or damaging in our lives. David encountered God's anger not because God was in a bad mood but because, as we shall see, David had fallen into the sin of pride, the most damaging of all sins. As a result, he needed the discipline of God in his life (Hebrews 12:4–11).

David learned that any period of discipline we experience is temporary; it has a limited timeframe and will not be severe enough to crush us. By contrast, God's blessing and favour are continuous and permanent, and we must not lose sight of this when times are hard. This knowledge is part of the encouragement that a chastened David has to offer us, and it will help us to hang in there when God is dealing with us.

The second half of verse 5 looks at disorientation from a human perspective. Here the temporary experience of weeping and darkness is contrasted with the rejoicing that comes with morning and the start of a new day. Weeping features prominently in the psalms of lament (6:6, 8; 39:12; 69:10) and it is part of Christian experience, whether it involves tears of repentance, of grief and loss, or of sorrow and anguish. Crying has its own healing properties, and we should not be afraid of expressing our emotions through our tears, no matter what our cultural background or gender.

There will be sad days in our walk with God, but these will be outnumbered by days when the sun is shining and we are rejoicing in God. We need to take hold of this promise when we are walking through the valley of deep darkness and our hearts are breaking. Light will come again; joy will be restored. Weeping is an overnight guest, but rejoicing is a permanent resident. I like what Brueggemann says here: 'The move from weeping to joy (cf. John 16:20) is as reliable as the move from night to daybreak. The power of daybreak is a new enactment of God's sovereignty, which is the ground of praise.'[31]

These are great insights to help us on our own pilgrim way, and they come to us courtesy of David's own experiences with God. In our own times of disorientation, we should ask God to show us what new insights we can gain. There is treasure in the darkness, and we will find it if we ask for understanding.

The foolishness of pride (vv. 6–7)

When I felt secure, I said,
'I shall never be shaken.'
O Lord, when you favoured me,
you made my mountain stand firm;
but when you hid your face,
I was dismayed.

David now looks back to the reason why he was disciplined by God—his pride. David had been chosen as a young boy for the purpose of God, and he had grown in power and authority because God had been with him, bringing him eventually to the position of king. Since he was 'a man after

God's own heart' (see Acts 13:22), the kingship was safe in his hands, and God made a covenant with him, promising that his kingdom would be established for ever (2 Samuel 7:11–16). Victory followed victory, success upon success. God's favour was upon him and his accomplishments piled up like a mountain before him. Adored by the people and blessed by God, he felt secure. That was when he fell into the trap of pride, thinking that his success was all his own doing, that he deserved it, that nothing could take it away from him—and he foolishly boasted, 'I will never be shaken' (v. 6).

There is no sin that stirs the righteous anger of God as does the sin of pride. It is the exact opposite of God's kingdom and therefore needed to be rooted out of David's life. Although God longs to be gracious to us and for his favour to be continually flowing towards us in blessing, here is one thing he will most definitely resist in our lives: 'God opposes the proud but gives grace to the humble' (1 Peter 5:5; James 4:6–10; Proverbs 3:34). If we allow ourselves to become complacent or self-satisfied, if we start to think that we deserve blessing or can manage by ourselves, we can be sure that sooner or later we will find the wind of God blowing in our face.

David identifies what happened in his case. God simply hid his face, and David's world came tumbling down. That was all it took to throw him into chaos, turmoil and dismay. When God's face was towards him, he was blessed; the moment God averted his gaze, David was floundering. This was, of course, no act of spite; God was not toying with him, treating him like a plaything. It was an act of love, designed to keep David in the place of blessing and to make him the kind of leader who would rule God's people well. We are not privy here to any specific expression of pride in David's life or, indeed, to the specifics of God's countering measures. All we need to know is that it was enough to bring David to his knees in humble repentance.

If there is one quality most commonly seen as the outcome of disorientation, it is a new humility. Pride is a deceptive sin: we rarely see it in ourselves, though others can often observe it. It is able to blind us and has so many subtle expressions that even the most self-aware can be caught off guard. Humility, likewise, is something we are not conscious of but should all seek, since it is a God-like characteristic. It is usually the unexpected byproduct of failure, sorrow and distress. God may have to bring us very low so that this grace can be formed in us: humiliation often leads to humility. A humble person knows that he or she owes everything to God.

Broken (vv. 8–9)

> To you, O Lord, I called;
> to the Lord I cried for mercy:
> 'What gain is there in my destruction,
> in my going down to the pit?
> Will the dust praise you?
> Will it proclaim your faithfulness?
> Hear, O Lord, and be merciful to me;
> O Lord, be my help.'

David's cry for help comes from a sincere place of brokenness before God. It is a cry for mercy, which means he is casting himself upon God, knowing that he has no currency with which to buy God's favour. Yes, he appears to be arguing his case, giving reasons why God might want to come to his aid (rather like the writer in Psalm 88:10–12), but this is not where his hope really lies. His hope is in the merciful character of God. David, the triumphant king, has been humbled. He needs help from a power greater than himself; he needs mercy in his time of need from one who will forgive his shortcomings. It brings him to a point of surrender, of offering up his sword to the true King. It is a moment of recognition that he is a created being, designed to live in dependency upon his Creator. It is the turning-point in his personal drama.

Here is the heart of the struggle that we all face in our times of disorientation. Disorientation has many expressions and is experienced in a variety of ways, but often at the centre of our struggle with God is the struggle for control: who is in charge? Some people, fortunately, surrender easily to God's loving reign over them; others fight to the bitter end, like Jacob wrestling with the stranger (Genesis 32:22–32), and for them the pain is perhaps greater. The same human heart is capable of the highest devotion and the most stubborn resistance, sometimes both at the same time. If God is to make our lives a blessing to others, though, we can be sure that he will meet us in the valley and wrestle with us until we surrender.

Transformation (vv. 11–12)

You turned my wailing into dancing;
you removed my sackcloth and clothed me with joy,
that my heart may sing to you and not be silent.
O Lord my God, I will give thanks to you for ever.

David now turns from thoughts of the past and his remembrance of his failure, to the present and his testimony of the transforming work of God in his life. These four lines, again, make up two couplets with parallel thoughts: verse 11 describes the change in David and verse 12 explains the reason and purpose behind God's activity in his life.

David's mood has been greatly altered by God's intervention. Because of his situation, he was wailing like a person distraught with grief; he was in sackcloth (whether literally or figuratively), like someone who is bereaved. Both pictures suggest a deep sorrow for his sin and foolishness, the kind of godly sorrow to which God responds in forgiving grace (2 Corinthians 7:9–10). Now, with his relationship with God re-established and on a right footing once more, his soul explodes with an exuberant joy that moves him into dancing, the kind of extravert expression of worship for which he had a reputation (2 Samuel 6:14). His relationship with God has been severely tested, but in the end God has shown himself to be compassionate and forgiving. David failed, and yet found himself still loved by the covenant-keeping God. Church leader Brian Mclaren remarks honestly that, in his experience, 'failure is what makes me more ready to learn than anything else. In fact, failure in itself is the lesson. Once you admit you are a failure you are strangely free... Everything is possible again when you have fought and struggled and been defeated, when you have come to zero'.[32]

Such a transformation is worthy in itself, but God is not interested in providing us with emotional highs. He is looking for more substantial change—for the adoption of praise as a way of life—and this is brought out in verse 12. Knowing what he now knows about God, and having experienced grace in the measure he has just received it, David's whole perspective is changed. Thanksgiving will become a lifestyle and his heart will not be silent but will sing God's praises.

Perhaps, previously, his worship had been conditional upon things going well in his life; now he will praise God, no matter what happens (Psalm 34:1–3; 103:1–5). Again Brueggemann summaries the situation well: 'Because of new life given only by God, silence is impossible. New life requires doxology, the end of sullenness, depression, numbness, despair.'[33]

Psalm 30 therefore fittingly brings us to the end of our journey through a selection of psalms that picture the movement from orientation into disorientation, and then from disorientation into reorientation. It is there in scripture to remind us that there is always hope, no matter how dark the night may seem. David went down into the valley and came up on the other side. His testimony and his inspired words are given to encourage us that we too can emerge from the darkness. They are recorded so that we can make them our own when we experience our own deliverance and want to give thanks to God.

* * *

Steve and Nwabisa are a couple in pastoral ministry in south London. Over the last few years they have had their own struggles in life, and, for Nwabisa in particular, this has meant a lot of heart searching and spiritual exploration.

15

Nwabisa's story

When we got married over seven years ago, we had a plan. We wanted to build a marriage with strong foundations and so we decided that we were going to spend the first two years adjusting to life together, enjoying each other and travelling, before children came along. We'd met in Italy, a South African and an Englishman, thanks to Oak Hall Christian holidays. After agonising about where we should base ourselves, God opened the door for us just two months before we got married. Steve was called to be the pastor of a church and we were provided with a lovely home. I soon started a new job and we were overwhelmed by God's blessings over our lives.

Time flew by, and two years later we could not wait to start a family. We tried for almost a year but nothing was happening, so we decided to visit our local surgery, just to be on the safe side. The GP we saw was not very tactful, to say the least. Before we had even fully explained why we had come, she jumped in with 'Oh, infertility problems!' To hear those words on that first visit was very upsetting, but not as discouraging as the many visits to the GP and fertility specialists that followed, with endless investigations and consultations about assisted pregnancy.

When the doctors told us our only realistic chance was to consider IVF, I froze. I couldn't breathe. I needed space to think and pray. We struggled because taking this route felt like 'playing God'. We had never imagined ourselves in this place. Why us? As we wrestled to make sense of our situation, we sought advice from mature, trusted Christian friends, who gently and wisely helped us through our struggles. In the end, we decided to go ahead with the IVF.

It was a complicated process with many potential obstacles, and we prayed at every step that, if this path was not right for us, God would close the door—but the doors kept opening. However, twelve days after a successful embryo transfer, I started bleeding. The embryos had failed to implant. There was nothing the doctors could do, and that was the end of that.

After a second cycle also failed, I felt abandoned by God. It seemed as if he had turned away from us, and I was devastated. I could not make sense of it. If this wasn't going to work, why hadn't he shut the doors in the first place? I had a constant pain in my heart and was overtaken by a deep longing to have my own baby. I functioned perfectly well on the outside but, inside, my world had fallen apart. I was in darkness. I lost my joy. There was no more colour in life. My life was altered—to what, I didn't know. I was confused. I was mystified by God. Where was he, what was he doing, why was he not answering our prayer?

For three years I was in mourning and wrestling with God. I kept company with many who had written much about suffering and unanswered prayer. I read, journalled and cried a lot. I ached for God to say something—anything. Now, it wasn't only about longing for a baby, but it was about my faith in crisis. Where was my God when I so desperately needed to hear from him? Church was too 'happy' and I was mourning. We sang songs like, 'Saviour, he can move the mountains', but I wrestled with God, tearfully telling him, 'My mountain is fixed in place, thank you very much!'

Then one day I said to my mentor, 'I'm tired of it. I can't seem to shake this sadness off. I just want to find joy in life again. Even if we don't get what we want, I just want to smile when I look at nature, like I used to.' Later that year, something gradually started happening within me. The aching began to ease. The longing for a baby loosened its grip on me. Don't get me wrong, I still wanted to have a child, but I was no longer so consumed by the pain.

When I saw my mentor again a year later, I said to him, 'My joy has returned, but I know I can't have done it. It must have been God. He has restored my joy.' After a great time of suffering, the Lord had taken away my garments of mourning and clothed me with joy. I was both grateful and deeply humbled. Now my soul is at peace and my joy is like a gentle bubbling brook. I still have difficult moments, but my joy runs deep, deeper than the joy I've known before. I came to know this through the experience of another potentially devastating setback.

We had been surprised by hope, as it had turned its face towards us when we least expected it. We were overjoyed when we suddenly learned that I was pregnant. However, our hope was shipwrecked in a moment, when, during a routine scan, the doctor told us that the foetus no longer had a heartbeat.

We were numb for several hours. We couldn't speak, think or pray. When eventually we could pray, the only words we could utter were, 'Lord, please hold us'. A few weeks later, we realised that he had heard that prayer. He held us. I didn't fall apart. The darkness didn't return. Instead, in our great sadness, the Lord gave me a picture. I saw the Lord holding both Steve and me on his knee and gently rocking us to sleep as he sang a lullaby over us. Suddenly, I felt a big teardrop landing on my cheek, and it wasn't mine—it was his. At that very moment, I knew that he was grieved by our loss just as much as we were. At that moment, I also knew that he had never left me, even during that long dark night of mourning. He was there in the shadows of my darkness, watching me as grief, pain and sadness enveloped me. He was there!

The depth of this joy is both cleansing and healing. The whole experience revealed to me that perhaps, deep down, my faith had been built on a false belief—that if I did the right things, God would give me what I asked for. When this didn't happen, I was shattered. It also taught me that I am not in control of life; life is a gift from God—a gift that is not perfect but is tainted by the human fallenness that affects us all. Sometimes life will throw a curveball at me, but I've come to accept that, even though I may not always get what I want, what I have instead leaves me broken but grateful. This lesson has humbled me and left me with a deep realisation of my dependence on God, and I'm learning to trust God, even when I don't understand.

16

Putting it all together

This has not been an easy book to write, and I guess it may not have been an easy book to read. I hope this realistic approach to spiritual formation has not been too disturbing, but, rather, has strengthened you for the very real challenges involved in seeking and attaining genuine spiritual growth. There is no easy path to maturity, no simple steps we can take to determine our development in God. God's invitation to deeper living is not for the shallow or the faint-hearted, but for the robust and the brave, those who are willing to walk where Jesus walked in the deep places of life.

Some years ago, Richard Foster made this perceptive remark: 'Superficiality is the curse of our age. The doctrine of instant satisfaction is a primary spiritual problem. The desperate need today is not for a greater number of intelligent people, or gifted people, but for deep people.'[34] More than three decades later, I believe that the problem for the church in the West remains the same, only more so, and the need for disciples of Christ to become deeper people is just as vital. This message is countercultural, for in both church and society the accent is on prosperity, comfort and the avoidance of suffering. The message that spiritual formation happens most commonly in the hard places of life, and that anyone who earnestly desires to know God more fully is likely to be led into times of difficulty, is unlikely to be universally welcomed or understood.

In the course of my writing I have been reminded of my own spiritual journey and made to reflect on how God has worked in me over the last 40 years. In some ways I feel I have led an easy life, mercifully free, so far, of major tragedy or misfortune. Yet, as I have written about some of the psalms of lament, I can see that my life has included many of the ingredients of spiritual formation mentioned here. I could easily have included my own story, for I too have been tested and tried. I have been through major conflict, and I know what it is to fail. I have been wrongly treated and felt the sting of injustice. I have been disappointed in God and known despair so great that I wanted to quit ministry once and for all. I have been hurt by those to whom I gave myself in pastoral care, and I have also made mistakes that have injured others. I have my own share of questions about God and his ways, and have been forced to rethink many of my most basic assumptions. In short, I too have been in the valley.

As I look back, I can see how God has used all of these 'negatives' to create something 'positive' in my life. He has taken me to deep places and there shaped and formed me into the person I am today—still far from complete but, I hope, more rounded and whole than I might otherwise have been. It seems that spiritual formation is best appreciated in retrospect. While we are going through difficulties, we don't recognise what God is doing in us, but later we can see how we have been changed. As Jesus said to Peter, 'You do not realise now what I am doing, but later you will understand' (John 13:7).

As we consider the spiritual movement from orientation to disorientation and then to reorientation, we may want to ask, 'What are the outcomes of such periods? What does spiritual transformation look like?' Spiritual formation is essentially about becoming Christ-like (Galatians 4:19), so that the characteristics we associate with him are increasingly seen in our lives. But what does this mean in practice? I want to suggest several ways in which transformation occurs in our lives, grouping them under three headings: character change, new understanding and a deepened experience.

Character change

One automatic response towards times of difficulty is to ask, 'What can I learn from this?' or 'What is God teaching me through this experience?' This is a common and understandable approach to finding meaning in our suffering, but it is not always helpful because, to be honest, sometimes we seem to be learning very little. A better question is 'Who am I *becoming* through this painful experience?' We may not be able to answer this question either, because, as we have seen, spiritual formation is best understood with hindsight, but at least it reminds us that God is more interested in shaping our hearts and forming our characters than in teaching us new things. We may be so absorbed by coping with life that we feel as if nothing is happening, but it is, and others may well be better placed to see the changes that pain and suffering have made in us.

To my mind, the greatest gift of the valley experience is that we are being made more humble. Humility is a truly Christ-like virtue, for Jesus said of himself, 'I am gentle and humble in heart' (Matthew 11:29). When God takes us into the deep places, I believe that his primary work is to humble us and release us from the grip of pride—pride expressed as arrogant self-confidence, a sense of superiority over others and the self-sufficiency of an independent spirit. By taking us out of our depth, God shows us that we cannot cope unaided and that we need outside help. The cry for mercy can only be made by someone who has reached the end of their tether and is humble enough to admit it. This often involves a painful and prolonged struggle until we yield ourselves to God, but, once reached, it becomes the place of transformation. When we have learned to live in humble dependence upon God, God is able to work through us, and we can then bear much fruit for him. Humility and dependency go hand in hand.

Alongside this, in the experience of the valley we develop a greater self-awareness. Pressure exposes our weaknesses and we become more realistic about ourselves, with a better understanding of our own hearts. This self-knowledge is also humbling. In the crucible of life, God refines our attitudes, liberating us from self-centredness and self-absorption so that we are free to think of others and care for them. Indeed, we can say that through personal suffering we are likely to become more compassionate, more considerate and more generous of heart. Having been shown our own shortcomings, we become more tolerant of weakness in others; having received grace, we are more able to give grace.

The periods of waiting that are characteristic of the valley experience help to form within us patience, perseverance and a stronger sense of trust in God. When we are called upon to go through dark times when there is little to reassure us, we are left with naked faith. All we can do is to hope in God. I love the advice that Daniel and Damaris were given by their African friends: 'When you can't see God's hand, trust his heart.' This simple saying enshrines a profound truth, that, ultimately, faith rests in the character of God. We can trust him in the bleakest of times simply because he is trustworthy. When we have come to know a trust like this, we have come to a place of spiritual maturity. 'Faith and hope work together to form a trusting disciple,' says Brennan Manning,[35] and nothing gives as much pleasure to God as to see that we trust him even in the darkness.

New understanding

Understanding is different from knowledge. Whereas knowledge is in the mind and has to do with facts and data, understanding is found in the heart and has to do with experience and insight. We do not gain new information through our valley experiences, but we do gain new understanding and wisdom. This is central in the process of transformation.

The 'need to know' is a deeply rooted human characteristic, especially for those brought up with a scientific worldview. Everything needs to have an explanation, and, once we can understand the reason for something, we feel in control of our world. This need easily transfers into our relationship with God, so that we assume we can understand him and how he works. Our instinctive approach is to systematise God and develop programmes that explain the Christian life in rational terms. This may be reassuring in the short term, but it is inadequate, for God is far too great to be captured or explained by any system of human thought. When we find ourselves in the valley and things are not working as we expected or predicted, we are in a dilemma. Suddenly the 'system' doesn't work and we are no longer in control, which is frightening and disturbing. This, however, is the moment when we are invited to step into a much greater understanding of God, which includes mystery and not-knowing: '"For my thoughts are not your thoughts, neither are your ways my ways,"' declares the Lord. "As the heavens are higher than the earth, so are my ways higher than your ways and my thoughts than your thoughts"' (Isaiah 55:8–9).

The idea that we could possibly 'fathom' God is, of course, ridiculous, but it is one of the most common reasons behind our struggle for faith. Once we can accept that we will not understand everything that God does, that he is beyond our comprehension and that it is all right to live without having an answer for everything, we are liberated into a realm where God is allowed once more to be God and we can be content to rest in his wisdom: 'Oh, the depth of the riches of the wisdom and knowledge of God! How unsearchable his judgements, and his paths beyond tracing out!' (Romans 11:33). In such a context we will still have questions, but they will no longer be barbed and damaging: we are content to live with them to see how they unfold over time, or we even become happy to continue without answers. This place where we are at home with mystery and not-knowing is one of the gifts that God gives us in the valley. God, we discover, can be trusted.

Understanding with the heart rather than with the mind helps us to cope with difficult situations that seem to make no sense. Many of us have a simplistic view of the love of God, for example. We assume that, if God loves us, he will never allow anything bad to happen to us. When things go wrong, we are thrown into turmoil and have to rethink our suppositions. Has God stopped loving me? If he loves me, why has he allowed this to happen to me? One thing we come to realise in the valley is that God's love is in no way sentimental. His love is strong and holy, and his unrelenting objective is to form the life of his Son within us. He is not weak in dealing with us, and will not be deflected from his purpose, no matter how much we whine (Romans 8:29; 2 Corinthians 13:3). As Paul writes in Romans 2:4, 'God is kind, but he's not soft. In kindness he takes us firmly by the hand and leads us into a radical life-change' (THE MESSAGE).

Steve McVey is an American Bible teacher and author. He tells how his three-year-old son awoke one night crying in agony. Realising it was something serious, Steve rushed the boy to the hospital, where he was diagnosed with an intestinal blockage. There was a need for some invasive procedures but, when the doctors started work, the boy began to pull away from the operating table in fear. Steve had no alternative but to hold him down while the doctor began the procedure. All the time, his son was crying out, 'Daddy, make him stop! Daddy, *why* won't you make him stop?' Steve began to cry as he hugged his son close and held him on the table. 'It's OK, son,' he said. 'Daddy's here with you. You must trust me, David. This is necessary. It's for your good. I'll hold you until it's over.'

Perhaps we have cried out to our heavenly Father concerning the circumstances of our life, 'Make it stop! Why won't you make it stop?' We may have felt abandoned, as the psalmist did, but God has not left us. McVey comments:

> *He may be holding you on the table so that you can't get up, but* **he is hugging you!** *He takes no pleasure in your pain, yet he loves you enough that if it takes pain to bring you to the place where he can accomplish his purpose for your good, he will allow it and keep you in it as long as necessary.*[36]

The silence and apparent inactivity of God that we sometimes experience in the valley do not mean that he is indifferent or uncaring. We begin to see that God, in his love for us, will complete the work he has begun in us, but he does so with tears and while holding us constantly in his love. This is the understanding of the heart, not of the mind. Remember what Nwabisa said: 'Suddenly, I felt a big teardrop landing on my cheek, and it wasn't mine—it was his.'

Deepened experience

When we emerge from a period of darkness or disorientation, we experience a surge of resurrection life. Once we have been humbled and purified, and have gained a new understanding of God and his ways, the Holy Spirit can take hold of us afresh to glorify God. He gives us a new song to sing (Psalm 33:3; 40:3; 96:1; 98:1; 144:9; 149:1), by which is meant a song (or message) that we know personally to be true. Now we are not simply using someone else's truth in a second-hand way, but we are expressing things we know to be true because we have experienced them. There is not only a new vitality to our praise but also a new authority. We now have a life-message to share with others because we have discovered truth for ourselves in the crucible of our experience. This makes for a very powerful testimony, and we often see the psalmists, for instance, sharing what they have discovered in the context of corporate worship (34:1–3; 40:9–10; 51:13; 89:1–2; 116:12–14). Now we can speak about God's grace, his faithfulness, his love and mercy with depth and meaning, for we have encountered them in the reality of our journey. This is not merely triumphalism, for the note of celebration includes a minor key. It is authentic praise that comes from a deep place within the heart of the worshipper who has met adversity and faced significant challenge, yet has come through transformed.

The valley experience is often a time for reassessment and review, for shedding inadequate ideas of God and receiving new revelation of what is important. Faith development requires us to let go of childish ways of thinking about God and adopt a more mature approach (1 Corinthians 13:11–12; Hebrews 6:1). In the valley we become better able to discern what is really central to our faith and what is less so. Such changes often occur during the period we call midlife (anywhere from 40 to 60 years of age), which is a natural transition period as well as a spiritually significant one for many people. During this period of upheaval and re-evaluation, we may be led to discover who we really are (our true identity as God's beloved children, as opposed to a false identity we have created through our achievements or status), and to find God's purpose for the second half of our lives (living not for success but for significance). Many of the psalms we have considered will express feelings recognisable to those going through a midlife transition, and, while the life–death–resurrection journey is not confined to the midlife years, there is certainly a correlation between the two.

It is Brueggemann's contention that, since life is never static either for individuals or communities, we are always moving either into orientation or out of orientation.[37] I am not sure I agree with this assertion. It seems to me that God, in his grace, allows us to have long periods of stability when things are settled and we are able to enjoy his goodness—just as the early church enjoyed seasons of well-being and peace (Acts 9:31). The deep experiences described in this book are, in fact, quite rare, and maybe only on a handful of occasions in the course of a lifetime will we find ourselves in such extreme positions. Yet these experiences are valid and can be expected, particularly in the lives of those who desire to know God more fully and to be used by him. Understanding the life–death–resurrection principle will mean that we are not taken by surprise when we find ourselves in a period of disorientation. Rather, we will have an inkling of what God is about and may be better equipped to come through these times as stronger people, more Christ-like and more effective in our service for God.

Questions for group discussion

These questions are designed for use in a group but could also be helpful for personal reflection.

Understanding psalms (Chapter 1)

- How well do you know the book of Psalms? What has been your experience of it so far in your Christian life?
- Do you have a favourite psalm? Why do you like this psalm in particular? How does it help and strengthen your faith?
- What do you think it is about the book of Psalms that makes it so universally popular?
- How is the book of Psalms used in the church you belong to? For example, how are the psalms used in worship? Do you ever read them together?
- Why not set yourself a challenge? Try to read through the whole book of Psalms in a month, not studying them in depth but getting a general impression of what they are about. Make a note of what you discover, and share it with others.

Understanding the book of Psalms (Chapter 2)

- The title of this book is *Deep Calls to Deep*, taken from Psalm 42:7. What does the author understand by this expression?

Why does he describe the Psalms as 'a handbook for spiritual formation'? (See Introduction, pages 8–9.)

- What do you understand by the term 'songs of lament'? Why are these psalms often neglected today? Do you think there is a valid place for the expression of sadness, grief and pain in worship?

- What are the three movements that we see when we consider the message of the Psalms as a whole? Consider how each one is helpful in understanding Christian experience.

- Try writing your own psalm—a poem, a prayer or a song. Think about the kind of psalm you want to write, whether one of praise or lament, thanksgiving or trust. Let your psalm arise out of your own circumstances if possible.

In the dark valley (Chapter 3)

- How do you understand the 'life–death–resurrection' pattern that the author describes? Think about John 12:24 as an illustration of this principle.

- Read Philippians 2:6–11 and consider how this same pattern is illustrated in the life of Jesus.

- Walter Bruggemann classifies the Psalms in a way that reflects this same pattern as a movement from orientation, through disorientation, and finally into reorientation. What do you understand by these terms? Is it a helpful way of reading the Psalms?

- Consider your own Christian experience. Do you see this pattern at work in your life or in the lives of others? Is it helpful to know that this kind of 'valley experience' is a normal part of the way God shapes and forms us?

Psalm 145 (Chapters 4 and 5)

This psalm, an 'alphabet of praise', reflects a season of orientation, when everything is normal and life is as it should be.

- Is praising God a way of life for you? What reasons for praise are given in the opening verses (vv. 1–3)?
- 'God is a great creator' (vv. 4–7). How does creation speak to us about the nature and character of God? How do you personally find God in the world around you?
- 'God is a gracious Lord' (vv. 8–9). What do these verses tell us about the nature and character of God? How do these truths encourage you and give confidence to you in the way you relate to God?
- 'God is a glorious king' (vv. 10–13). How does belief in the sovereignty of God steady our faith in times of storm? What strength do you personally derive from being part of his kingdom?
- 'God is a generous provider' (vv. 13–16). How have you experienced God's provision in your life? What do you think it means to live with a sense of daily dependence upon him?
- 'God is a guardian protector' (vv. 17–20). What comfort can you take from the awareness that God is near, listening to your prayer and watching over you?
- What is your overall feeling or impression as you meditate on this psalm (v. 21)?
- How does Mags's story speak to you?

Psalm 130 (Chapters 6 and 7)

This psalm takes us into the season of disorientation by helping us explore the theme of personal failure.

- Think about the nature of sin as failure—either to do what is right or not to do what is wrong. What has been your experience, before you became a believer and since knowing God personally?
- How does sin bring people down into the depths (vv. 1–2)? Consider this question either from your own experience or from the experience of people whom you know or know about. How does serious failure provide an opportunity for spiritual growth and the deepening of faith?
- Meditate on the words, 'But with you there is forgiveness' (v. 4). How do they speak to you? How do they apply to your life right now? Have you been 'thoroughly' forgiven?
- Waiting is a common feature of disorientation (vv. 5–6). Why is God said to be 'never in a hurry'? Of the different aspects of waiting described in Chapter 6, which in your experience has been the most difficult?
- We often want to protect ourselves from the embarrassment of failure, and to avoid the risk of sharing our struggles with others. How can being real and authentic not only strengthen the one who shares but also bring blessing to others (vv. 7–8)?
- What have you learned (a) about yourself, and (b) about God, from any experience you have had of failure?
- How does Avril's story speak to you?

Psalms 42 and 43 (Chapters 8 and 9)

Here we look at the increasingly common problem of depression, especially 'spiritual' depression—the darkness we may experience during a time of disorientation, when we do not understand what God is doing.

- What classic symptoms of depression can be seen in these two psalms? What, according to the author, may have been the reason for this despair?
- What has been your own experience of depression or emotional struggle? Have you ever felt parched and dry? Overwhelmed and unable to cope? Abandoned by God and neglected? If so, how did you cope? What helped, and what didn't?
- From your experience, what has been the general attitude towards depression in society and in the church?
- Meditate on the 'chorus of faith' (42:5, 11; 43:5). Remind yourself of the steps outlined by the writer, based on these verses, by which we can begin to resist the overwhelming pull towards despair.
- What do you think the psalmist learned from his experience of depression? How might he, with hindsight, answer his own questions in 42:2, 9 and 43:2?
- What can you take from this psalm to (a) strengthen yourself, and (b) help others?
- How does Rick's story speak to you?

Psalm 69 (Chapters 10 and 11)

This psalm takes us to an even deeper place of disorientation as the writer wrestles with the injustice of what has happened to him and God's apparent refusal to respond to his cry for help.

- Have you ever been falsely accused of wrongdoing or treated unjustly? Do you know others who have? How does suffering unjustly make us feel?
- Try to piece together, from verses 1–12, something of David's situation and the way it affected his relationship with God.
- Strangely, this psalm is one of the most often quoted in the New Testament, and it is full of echoes of Christ's experience. With the help of Chapter 10 in the book, identify the places in the psalm where we can see the presence of Jesus. How does it help to know that 'in the depths' we have an opportunity to (a) get to know Christ better, (b) become one with him in his suffering, and (c) experience his wonderful presence and sustaining grace?
- Do you find it difficult to pray when you are under pressure? What motivated David to reach out to God despite his pain and bewilderment (vv. 13–18)? How can this encourage us?
- The psalmist finds himself in a very lonely and isolated place. How might a person seek to find solace inappropriately at such a time? What might be better ways to meet our need for comfort when we are emotionally down?
- What is your response to the angry outburst in verses 22–29? How do you deal with your own anger? Why do you think we have passages like this in the Bible?
- Notice how the psalm ends with praise (vv. 30–36). What does this say to us?
- How does Samara's story speak to you?

Psalm 88 (Chapters 12 and 13)

There is no psalm that takes us to a deeper place of disorientation than this. Of all the songs of lament, this is the saddest, yet God is in it and we can learn from it.

- What is your reaction to this psalm? Is it the kind of psalm you would prefer not to read? Does it challenge your understanding of the Christian life?
- What do you understand by 'the dark night of the soul'? How does this psalm reflect this experience of apparent abandonment by God? See verses 3–8, 10–12 and 14–18.
- An experience like the one described in this psalm is very rare, but have you ever felt any of these emotions yourself, even if in a lesser way? What can you learn from Mother Teresa's experience of darkness?
- The psalmist shows a striking commitment to the spiritual discipline of prayer (vv. 1–2, 9, 13). Why is it important to stick to basic 'holy habits' even when they seem to offer no reward or we don't feel like doing them?
- Consider some of the suggested reasons for the value of a psalm like this and its place in the scriptures. Do any of them seem especially valid to you? Do you have other thoughts?
- 'The darkness is my closest friend' (v. 18). This seems a very sad note on which to end the psalm, but how might it be a positive statement? How can we befriend the darkness?
- How does the story of James and Debbie speak to you?

Psalm 30 (Chapters 14 and 15)

At last we come out of the darkness of disorientation and emerge into the light of the phase known as reorientation. This is a time for thanksgiving and for sharing testimony of God's deliverance.

- What testimony can David give after his experience 'in the depths' (vv. 1–3). What metaphors does he use to describe his experience? How would you describe his feelings?
- What lesson has he learned through his time of testing (vv. 4–5)? With whom does he share his story? How do you understand the truth of verse 5?
- As he looks back on his period of disorientation (vv. 6–7), David acknowledges that it was his pride that got him into trouble. In what ways had David's pride displayed itself? Why is pride such an enemy to spiritual growth? How can we cultivate its alternative, which is humility?
- In verses 8–9, David remembers how God humbled him and brought him low. His experience of brokenness allowed God to work in his life. How do you understand this idea of 'brokenness'? What is it, and what is it not?
- David received mercy from God (vv. 8–9). Why is mercy the gift that we need most from God? How might receiving mercy affect us for good?
- Finally, in verses 11–12, David allows himself to rejoice in all that God has done for him. What changes had taken place in his life? How do these verses reflect the fact that he is now in the place of reorientation?
- How does Nwabisa's story speak to you?

Putting it all together (Chapter 16)

- The author says that this was not an easy book to write, and he imagines that it will not have been an easy read. What has been your overall response to what you have read in the book, and in the Psalms?
- How do you respond to the message of the book that spiritual formation often takes place in the hard places of life, and that anyone who desires to know God more fully may well be led into times of difficulty?
- The first potential outcome of the valley experience is that it produces a change in character. What might this look like in the life of an individual? What are some of the key changes that God is looking for?
- A second benefit is a new understanding. How might God be seeking to change our thinking? Why might 'not knowing' become more important to us as we mature in Christ?
- The third benefit suggested in this chapter concerns a deepened experience. How is the 'new song' different from the old one? In what other ways might we be shaped into becoming 'deeper' people? What do you think this means?
- What one significant insight have you gained from this study, and how might you be different as a result?

Classification of various psalms

This is by no means a comprehensive categorisation of every psalm. Some psalms are not easy to classify and may not appear here, while some can be placed in more than one category. There is no definitive listing, and classification is a subjective matter anyway, to some extent, but it serves to highlight some of the different types of psalm that we meet as we read the book of Psalms.

Praise psalms (hymns)

8, 29, 33, 47, 65, 66, 68, 93, 96, 97, 98, 99, 100, 103, 104, 105, 106, 111, 113, 114, 117, 134, 135, 136, 145, 146, 147, 148, 149, 150

Psalms of lament

Individual: 3, 4, 5, 6, 7, 11, 13, 17, 22, 27, 30, 31, 32,, 35, 51, 63, 69, 71, 91, 102, 130
Community: 44, 60, 74, 77, 79, 80, 83, 85, 90, 94, 123, 126, 137

Psalms of thanksgiving

Individual: 18, 30, 31, 32, 40, 66, 92, 116, 118, 120
Community: 65, 66, 107, 118, 124, 129

Psalms of trust

Individual: 4, 16, 23, 27, 62, 73
Community: 90, 115, 123, 124, 125, 126

Psalms of remembrance (Israel's history)

44, 68, 77, 78, 80, 95, 99, 104, 105, 106, 107, 114, 135, 136, 137

Wisdom psalms (including those centred on the Torah)

1, 32, 34, 37, 49, 73, 78, 91, 112, 119, 127

Kingship or royal psalms

Earthly king: 2, 18, 20, 21, 45, 72, 89, 101, 110, 132, 144
Heavenly king: 47, 93, 95, 96, 97, 98, 99

Bibliography

Commentaries on the book of Psalms

Philip Greenslade, *Songs for All Seasons* (CWR, 2003)

John Goldingay, *Songs from a Strange Land* (IVP, 1978)

Geoffrey W. Grogan, *Psalms* (Eerdmans, 2008)

Derek Kidner, *Psalms 1—72* (IVP, 1973)

Derek Kidner, *Psalms 73—150* (IVP, 1975)

Phil Moore, *Psalms* (Monarch, 2013)

A.B. Rhodes, *Psalms* (SCM, 1960)

Michael F. Ross, *The Light of the Psalms* (Christian Focus, 2006)

Michael Sadgrove, *I Will Trust In You* (SPCK, 2009)

James W. Sire, *Thirsting for God* (SU, 2005)

John Stott, *Favourite Psalms* (Monarch, 2003)

Derek Tidball, *Signposts* (IVP, 2009)

Arthur Weiser, *The Psalms* (SCM, 1962)

Michael Wilcock, *Psalms 1—72* (IVP, 2000)

Michael Wilcock, *Psalms 73—150* (IVP, 2000)

Books about the Psalms

Walter Brueggemann, *The Message of the Psalms* (Augsburg, 1984)

Walter Brueggemann, *Praying the Psalms* (Paternoster, 2007)

C. Hassell Bullock, *Encountering the Book of Psalms* (Baker Academic, 2001)

Sotirios Christou, *The Psalms* (Phoenix, 2010)

David J. Cohen, *Why, O Lord?* (Paternoster, 2013)

Tremper Longman III, *How to Read the Psalms* (IVP, 1988)

James L. Mays, *The Lord Reigns* (John Knox Press, 1994)

Simon Stocks, *Using the Psalms for Prayer through Suffering* (Grove, 2007)

Books about suffering

Jane Grayshon, *Treasures of Darkness* (Hodder & Stoughton, 1996)

Pete Greig, *God on Mute* (Kingsway, 2007)

Timothy Keller, *Walking with God through Pain and Suffering* (Hodder & Stoughton, 2013)

Brian Kolodiejchuk, *Mother Teresa: Come be my light* (Rider, 2007)

Cecil Murphy, *Seeking God's Hidden Face* (IVP, 2001)

Henri Nouwen, *Can You Drink This Cup?* (Ave Maria Press, 1996)

Henri Nouwen, *Turn My Mourning into Dancing* (Word, 2001)

Notes

1 Tremper Longman III, *How to Read the Psalms* (IVP, 1988), pp. 11–12.
2 See *How to read the Psalms*, ch. 7.
3 David J. Cohen, *Why, O Lord?* (Paternoster, 2013), p. 11.
4 C. Hassell Bullock, *Encountering the Book of Psalms* (Baker Academic, 2001), p. 63.
5 Bullock, *Encountering the Book of Psalms*, p. 71.
6 James L. Mays, *The Lord Reigns* (Westminster John Knox, 1994), p. 62.
7 Geoffrey Grogan, *Psalms* (Eerdmans, 2008), p. 27.
8 Cohen, *Why, O Lord?* pp. 2–3.
9 Walter Brueggemann, *The Message of the Psalms* (Augsburg, 1982), pp. 10, 20.
10 Brueggemann, *Message of the Psalms*, p. 20.
11 Brueggemann, *Message of the Psalms*, p. 30.
12 James W. Sire, *Thirsting for God* (SU, 2005), pp. 34–35.
13 Michael Wilcock, *Psalms 73—150* (IVP, 2000), p. 239.
14 Derek Kidner, *Psalms 73—150* (IVP, 1975), p. 446.
15 World Health Organisation website: www.who.int/topics/depression
16 Derek Kidner, *Psalms 1—72* (IVP, 1973), p. 182.
17 Martyn Lloyd-Jones, *Spiritual Depression: Its causes and cure* (Pickering & Inglis, 1965), p. 20.
18 Grogan, *Psalms*, p. 128.
19 Timothy Keller, *Walking with God through Pain and Suffering* (Hodder & Stoughton, 2013), pp. 242, 245.
20 Michael Wilcock, *Psalms 1—72* (IVP, 2000), p. 241.
21 The other imprecatory psalms are 35; 55; 59; 79; 109 and 137.
22 Brueggemann, *Message of the Psalms*, p. 78.
23 Gordon Mursell (ed.), *The Story of Christian Spirituality* (Lion, 2001), p. 211.
24 Brian Kolodiejchuk, *Mother Teresa: Come be my light* (Rider, 2007), pp. 1–2.

25 Quoted by Alexander Ryrie, *Silent Waiting* (Canterbury Press, 1999), p. 171.

26 David Benner, *Soulful Spirituality* (Brazos, 2011), p. 136.

27 Benner, *Soulful Spirituality*, p. 139.

28 Kolodiejchuk, *Mother Teresa*, p. 208.

29 Jane Grayshon, *Treasures of Darkness* (Hodder & Stoughton, 1996), p. 138.

30 Kidner, *Psalms 73—150*, p. 317.

31 Brueggemann, *Message of the Psalms*, p. 127.

32 Brian D. Mclaren, *Naked Spirituality* (Hodder & Stoughton, 2010), pp. 208–209.

33 Brueggemann, *Message of the Psalms*, p. 127.

34 Richard Foster, *Celebration of Discipline* (Hodder & Stoughton, 1980), p. 1.

35 Brennan Manning, *Ruthless Trust* (SPCK, 2002), p. 87.

36 Steve McVey, *Grace Rules* (Harvest House, 1998), pp. 36–37.

37 Brueggemann, *Message of the Psalms*, p. 125.

An introduction to spiritual mentoring, for those who are exploring this aspect of discipleship or embarking on training for ministry as a mentor within their church. Tony Horsfall explains, through the metaphor of the journey, both process and purpose—what mentoring means, its benefits to all involved, and how to explore the call to be a mentor to others. Written primarily for those unfamiliar with spiritual direction, it will encourage you to prioritise your own spiritual growth as well as consider whether God may be calling you to be a 'soul friend'.

Mentoring for Spiritual Growth
Sharing the journey of faith
Tony Horsfall
978 1 84101 562 0 £6.99

brfonline.org.uk